A WOMEN'S 10-WEEK STUDY OF
DEUTERONOMY 1–11

REMEMBER THIS
A Work of Heart

Monica J. Butler

college press
Joplin, Missouri

Remember This:
A Work of Heart

Copyright © 2024 College Press Publishing
www.collegepress.com

Cover Design by Karis Pratt

Interior Design by Mandie Tepe

All Scripture quotations, unless indicated, are taken from The Holy Bible: The New International Version®, NIV®. Copyright ©1973, 1978, 1984, 2011 by Biblica, Inc.™ Used by permission of Zondervan. All rights reserved worldwide. www.zondervan.com The "NIV" and "New International Version" are trademarks registered in the United States Patent and Trademark Office by Biblica, Inc.™

The Exodus Bible map has been provided by and is used by permission from MANNA Bible Maps at www.biblemaps.com.

ISBN 978-0-89900-131-9 (7 x 10)
ISBN 978-0-89900-132-6 (8.5 x 11)

Monica Butler has written an accessible and insightful guide to Deuteronomy 1-11. Each group study session includes information that provides context for reading Deuteronomy and a steady stream of questions to encourage reflection and application. The workbook format enables the student to do these things. Here is a resource that facilitates a meaningful encounter with words from the Lord meant to shape the hearts of his people.

—**Dr. Trevor Cochell**
Rocky Mountain School
of Ministry and Theology

TESTIMONIALS FROM WOMEN WHO HAVE GONE THROUGH THE STUDY

Monica's study of Deuteronomy (chapters 1-11) is academic and reflective. Exploring the covenant love of God for Israel and future generations, loving Him with all our heart, learning His commands, and modeling and teaching our children to obediently walk in His ways have helped me see God's amazing love and faithfulness! This study is full of rich insights and extensive research you will want to experience!

—**Diana R.**

"Who would have thought there could be a well-written study for the book of Deuteronomy that is also interesting, thought-provoking, historically accurate, and completely applicable to our lives today? Praise the Lord! That study is here, and it's an absolute joy! Time after time, the choice stood before the Israelites Will they remember and obey in that circumstance? Or forget and fulfill their own desires. God was at work in their hearts big time! And likewise, He's at work in our hearts today."

—**Lara K.**

"Monica has truly been a blessing to my life. God has gifted her with the talents of speaking and writing biblical truth. Monica meets women where they are in their walk with Jesus, whether a new believer or a mature Christian. She is eager to research a Bible text to clear up Bible study confusion, and often times refers to herself as a "Bible Nerd"! Monica has a servant's heart and emphasizes pointing others to Christ and encouraging those to deepen their relationship with Christ.

This Deuteronomy Bible study has enlightened me and made me willing to check out the Old Testament further. It piqued my interest to explore the lessons that Moses and the Israelites experienced as God led them to the Promised Land.

The title of this study leans into this verse in Psalms, "Create in me a pure heart, O God, and renew a steadfast spirit within me" (Psalm 51:10). God is molding and refining our hearts to be more like Him.

—**Vonny R.**

"I immediately accepted the invitation to join this Deuteronomy study. I love history, in general, and I find biblical history fascinating. Yet, I had no idea what a huge blessing was in store for me! I have spent most of my life studying the New Testament – Christ's birth, life, death, and ascension. Studying Deuteronomy gave me a clearer and deeper understanding of these truths. As I continue to read and study Scripture, the teachings of the Old Testament book of Deuteronomy are a constant revelation and testimony to who Jesus is and all He has done. I am always reminded that "the volume of the Book" (Hebrews 10) is written of Jesus Christ."

—**Mauranda D.**

"This Bible study has been a complete blessing and an in-depth look at a holy, just, and compassionate God who "leads," "loves," "disciplines," "delivers," "protects," "reminds," and "continues to make a way for His people "through the desert.

This Bible study gives a rich history of Israel as God teaches the importance of His law and the consequences of obedience and disobedience to His perfect word. It has been a precious reminder to me to love God with all my heart, soul, and might to teach my children (& grandchildren) diligently the ways of Christ! This will be a Bible study I will go back through regularly to "only take care, and keep my soul diligently." Deut. 4:9 It has been a reminder to hold on to and lay up God's Word in my heart and soul! May God bless every heart who goes through this study as they consider how they too might submit a stubborn will to the heart of a faithful, loving, and reliable God!"

—**Kari W.**

"Since Jesus and NT writers quoted so frequently from Deuteronomy, it is crucial to become familiar with it. This group study enables that familiarity by providing tools to put commands into practice & to "remember." It facilitates sharing and openness among women, leading to lasting friendships. There is humor as "hornet" and "tablets that YOU BROKE" are discussed. Studying several Jewish traditions makes the text come alive and increases understanding. The same commands "proclaimed in a loud voice" to Israel show His glory and majesty to us as we seek to love Him, obey Him, and live long lives (eternal lives)."

—**Lynn H.**

When I was invited to this Bible study on Deuteronomy, I thought, "What does *that* have to do with my life?" As it turns out, it has EVERYTHING to do with my life. As we entered this study of God's people wandering in the desert, I was in a "desert" season. The constant refrain, "Do not forget to remember," became the cry of my heart as I practiced patient obedience to God's word. Monica's thoughtful presentation of this Old Testament book ignited my desire to study and learn more about the Old Testament. Studying the foundation of God's promises to His people is incredibly eye-opening as you continue to see His love and care for His people reflected throughout all of Scripture.

—**Sandi M.**

"Honestly, I didn't know what to expect from this study. I had read through Deuteronomy before but it didn't "stick." Once I started it and went over the discussion questions with the group, I learned so much about God's foundational truths. It's made the further studies I've been a part of more meaningful because I see the connection between the Old and New Testament."

—**Sanji H.**

WELCOME!

I'm so glad you're here! Time spent in God's Word is always time well spent, and time spent with others seeking to do the same is especially good!

I'm not sure where you are in your acquaintance with the Bible, but it is my hope that over the course of the next ten weeks your familiarity with, your understanding of, and your love for God's Word will grow in mighty ways. I especially hope that you find an incredible fondness for the rich teachings of the Old Testament and how they inform and enhance all you may have learned in the New Testament, and certainly all you consider in your life today.

As we walk through the text, we will assuredly walk through some passages that are encouraging, some that are mysterious, and even some that are disturbing, but we can be sure that all are rooted in the unchanging character of God Himself. It is my prayer that spaces that seem difficult right now may seem less so over time, and that the great faithfulness of the God who is the same yesterday, today, and forever will be made even more evident throughout our wilderness journey together.

I'm honored to meet with you here in this space and I'm eagerly praying for each of you as you say "yes" to digging into the text of Deuteronomy.

Let's hear from God, get to know His heart, and find our hearts forever changed!

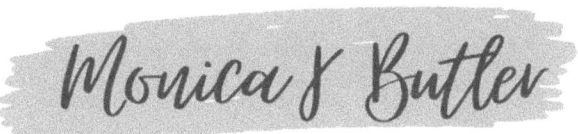

TABLE OF CONTENTS

Introduction: Heart of Deuteronomy/Context 9

Week One: Remember: Rescue & Rebellion...How Did Israel Get Here? (Ch 1) 12

Week Two: Remember: Wanderings & War...Moses Will Not Enter (Ch 2-3) 31

Week Three: Remember: Respond, Repent, Find Refuge (Ch 4) 49

Week Four: Remember: Take These Words to Heart (Ch 4:44-49 & Ch 5) 69

Week Five: Remember: A Work of Heart (Ch 6) 91

Week Six: Remember: A Chosen Nation (Ch 7) 109

Week Seven: Remember: The Lord Himself Has Given Everything (Ch 8) 127

Week Eight: Remember: Not Righteous, But Rebellious, and Yet Redeemed (Ch 9) 145

Week Nine: Remember: God's Law Preserved, God's Care Extended (Ch 10) 166

Week Ten: Remember Today: Love the Lord & His Law (Ch 11) 181

Final Thoughts 198

Bibliography 200

Leader Tips/Helps 203

Practical Tips/Suggestions for Small Group Discussion Leaders 205

Suggested Flow for Weekly Group Study Meetings 207

Appendix/Map 208

INTRODUCTION
Getting Started

If the Old Testament has a heartbeat, it may well be the book of Deuteronomy.[1] This fifth book of the Old Testament canon, the last book of the Jewish Pentateuch, offers a pastoral approach to the history of Israel. It offers up a summary of sorts of the previous four books, as a "preached law," seeking to give the nation of Israel reminders of the laws they had been taught, with a prophetic urgency to action.[2]

Before we dive into any Bible study, we want to best understand the context of the passages/books we are seeking to understand. We always want to consider things such as: the author, the time period and historical context in which the writing originated, the original audience and their cultural context, the literary context of the writing, and the context within the canon of Scripture. We will seek to consider those contexts in this introduction section.

First, the book of Deuteronomy has traditionally been understood to have been authored by Moses. Over time, various scholars have suggested various theories for multiple authors over multiple timeframes, but the predominant accepted author has been identified as Moses (affirmed by Jesus Himself and by the book of Deuteronomy itself in 31:9 and 31:24).[3] Indeed, Moses can be "confirmed as the dominant, principal, and determinant voice in the book."[4] For our study's purposes, we will work from this assumption.

The timing of Deuteronomy's authoring has not been as easily determined and has been debated amongst scholars. The best potential dating points to a period between 1446-1269 BC, based upon the book of Exodus, and the correlation the document holds to ancient Near Eastern treaties utilized from 1400-1200 BC.[5] That said, one potential reason scholars may find it difficult to date Deuteronomy is because it has been said to have "a timeless quality that speaks clearly to each generation."[6] We will, no doubt, experience that timeless quality as we study together.

---

[1] Tidball, Derek. *The Message of the Living God: His Glory, His People, His World.* (Downers Grove, IL: InterVarsity Press, 2000), 166.

[2] Wright, Christopher J.H. *Understanding the Bible Commentary Series: Deuteronomy.* (Grand Rapids, MI: Baker Books, 1996), 21.

[3] Oberst, Bruce. *Bible Study Textbook Series: Deuteronomy.* (Joplin, MO: College Press, 1968), 3-4.

[4] Hill, Andrew E. and John A. Walton, editors. *A Survey of the Old Testament, Third Edition.* (Grand Rapids, MI: Zondervan, 2009), 165.

[5] Walton, John H., general editor. *Zondervan Illustrated Bible Backgrounds Commentary, Vol 1: Genesis, Exodus, Leviticus, Numbers, Deuteronomy.* (Grand Rapids, MI: Zondervan, 2009), 420.

[6] Kroeger, Catherine Clark and Mary J. Evans. *The IVP Women's Bible Commentary.* (Downers Grove, IL: InterVarsity Press,

The original audience for this book would have been the nation of Israel. Deuteronomy was a series of sermons Moses preached before the nation of Israel, as they stood opposite the long-awaited Promised Land of Canaan. This generation had been under 20 years old when leaving Egypt or had been born in the 40 years of wilderness wandering that followed Israel's deliverance from slavery. Moses took this occasion to recount Israel's history, and the statutes and commands from their God, to best prepare the nation to "go in and take possession of the land."

The book of Deuteronomy has been likened to the suzerain-vassal treaties of the ancient Near East timeframe.[7] In this context, God would be seen as the suzerain (sovereign ruler) and Israel would be seen as the vassal (servant/submitting party). The many commands and consequences for obedience/disobedience correlate to this literary style. (We will explore this further in the second volume of this study.)

Within the canon of Scripture, the book of Deuteronomy has been likened to a "literary and theological hinge" which "ties together what precedes to what follows," specifically the books of the Pentateuch to the books of history that follow.[8] It serves as a repetition or review of the law that had been previously shared in the first four books of the canon, while doing so with a call to obey as a new way of life in response to their redemption. This is in keeping with the rest of Scripture which scholar Sandra Richter says, "in all its parts is intended to communicate to humanity the realities of redemption."[9] This book fits the bill.

And, because I'm an Old-Testament enthusiast, and I long for you to be one, too, I would be remiss to not pass along another remarkable observation by Richter about the Old Testament as a whole. She says that two-thirds of the "redemption story" the Bible is seeking to communicate is contained within the Old Testament![10] We give a lot of credence to the idea that God's story of redemption is mainly contained within the gospel writings and epistles within the New Testament, but statistics tell us otherwise!

As we walk through the text of Deuteronomy, we will see many repeated words, phrases, concepts, and truths. We will want to pause and notice these. We will want to take note of the many ways we see these repetitions (repeated so we would remember and not forget) and to take care to hear what the Lord is telling Israel, and so telling us.

The book of Deuteronomy is a call to hear the words of Moses (as the words from the Lord) and allow them to transform and conform our hearts to the will of the Lord. We don't want to miss what the Lord is telling us, in our minds and in our hearts. We want to heed the call to better

---

2002), 88.

[7] Walton, John H., general editor. *Zondervan Illustrated Bible Backgrounds Commentary, Vol 1: Genesis, Exodus, Leviticus, Numbers, Deuteronomy,* 420.

[8] Arnold, Bill T. and Bryan E. Beyer, editors. *Encountering the Old Testament: A Christian Survey.* (Grand Rapids, MI: Baker Books, 1999), 151.

[9] Richter, Sandra L. *The Epic of Eden: A Christian Entry into the Old Testament.* (Downers Grove, IL: InterVarsity Press, 2008), 15.

[10] Ibid., 16.

live out the will and Word of the Lord. We want to live out our theology (a fancy word for the study of the nature of God) and see ourselves and others around us changed.

In Deuteronomy we are called to hear and obey, so that we might understand the character of God, which forms the heart and identity of His people.[11] This is at the heart of a lived-out theology. As we work through the book of Deuteronomy, it is my prayer that we will all approach each text with this goal in mind: *Remember This: A Work of Heart.*

For practical help purposes:

1) This study has been developed relying upon the New International Version translation of the Bible. You can certainly study using other translations, but if you find yourself stuck on a reflection or fill-in-the-blank question, you may want to consult the passage in the NIV translation to see if that helps.

2) The study has been broken into ten weekly sessions of individual homework. Each week has five days of personal homework. The amount of time required for each day's work varies, depending upon the text considered. The homework is best considered in a daily approach, but it is agreeable to working through multiple days in one sitting.

3) Consider consulting the cross-reference sections of your hard copy Bibles and online Bible application programs. You may find yourself running onto trails you did not anticipate, but the very nature of this book and its overview of multiple narratives and historical context demanded selective inclusion of other texts within this study. There were many texts that were not included simply because of time and space. I encourage you to have fun connecting proverbial dots in your study time.

4) I encourage you to participate in this study as a part of a small group community. Personal study is of great value, but study and discussion within a community is discipleship at its finest (and a reflection of the book itself in its emphasis on community). Share and encourage one another with what you are learning, and you will see incredible benefit and growth! Refer to the Leader Tips/Helps section in the back of this workbook for guidance to make the most of your group experience.

And, with all of this in mind, let's prepare to begin our study together!

---

[11] Wiersbe, Warren W. *The Bible Exposition Commentary Old Testament: The Pentateuch, Genesis-Deuteronomy.* (Colorado Springs, CO: David C. Cook, 2001), 384.

WEEK ONE

Remember: Rescue & Rebellion… How Did Israel Get Here?

CHAPTER 1

As we considered in our introductory session, the book of Deuteronomy is a call for God's people to hear from the Lord Himself. It's a call for them to prepare their hearts before entering the Promised Land. It's a call from a dying man to offer up counsel for a nation to consider all they need to know before he departs from their presence.

"These are the words…" (*devarim* in Hebrew) is the title of this book in the Jewish Bible, and this week we will begin to dig deeply into these words.[12] We'll consider what they meant to the nation of Israel *then* as they prepared to cross the Jordan and what they mean to each of us on "this side of the Jordan" *now*.

---

[12] Schultz, Samuel J. *Deuteronomy: The Gospel of Love*. (Chicago, IL: The Moody Bible Institute, 1971), 13.

DAY ONE

Command to Leave Horeb
(Deuteronomy 1:1-8)

Let's dig right into the text of Deuteronomy and hear the words of Moses.

~ • ~ • ~

Read Deuteronomy 1:1-8.

Here, the text gives us background information about the place and time of Moses' declarations to Israel as he prepares to unpack their history and "how they got there."

He is speaking to Israel while east of the Jordan in the Arabah (a wilderness valley along the Jordan and on the eastern edge of the Dead Sea).[13] This is a space we can readily identify and recognize. But Arabah is only one name within a list of many others. Before we can move further into the text we must pause to consider where these other locations were in ancient Israel.

Therein lies a puzzle that scholars have long debated. Theologians in Judaism and Christianity have held varying views on this list. Some rabbinical traditions have seen these as spaces where Moses had previously taught God's commands, but the lack of some notable spaces (Mt. Horeb/Mt. Sinai for one) makes this less likely.[14] Other rabbinical traditions have seen them as "veiled rebukes" to Israel, recounting spaces that held emotional recognition for those hearing Moses.[15] This line of thinking may hold some merit worth considering

Rabbinical teaching in *The Chumash* (a Jewish commentary from the rabbinical writings) presents these considerations for these otherwise less understood geographical places.

> **Suph**: This may refer to the Red Sea, and so point to the Israelites complaining that Yahweh (the name the Israelites called their God) had brought them through the Red Sea and to the wilderness to die. "Were there no graves in Egypt?" is the question they asked in Exodus 14:11.[16]

---

[13] *NIV Cultural Study Backgrounds Bible*. (Grand Rapids, MI: Zondervan, 2016), 293.

[14] Ben-Gad HaCochen, Dr. David. "Where in the Transjordan Did Moses Deliver His Opening Address?" TheTorah.com. (2018), 6. https://thetorah.com/article/where-in-the-transjordan-did-moses-deliver-his-opening-address

[15] Scherman, Rabbi Nosson and Rabbi Meir Zlotovitz. *The Stone Edition: The Chumash*. (Brooklyn NY: Mesorah Publications, Ltd, 2012), 939.

[16] Ibid.

Paran: The spies (to survey the land in Numbers 13-14; we will learn more about them soon) were sent from Paran.[17]

Tophel and Laban: There are no places known by these names, but the word Laban means "white" and rabbinical tradition suggests this may refer to the white color of manna (the bread Yahweh fed the Israelites in the wilderness), and Tophel can correlate with a Hebrew word that means "slander." Thus, both spaces may refer to two places the Israelites complained about the manna (Numbers 10:12, 11:6).[18]

Hazeroth: Korah's (a leader in Israel) rebellion against Moses took place at or near Hazeroth (Numbers 16:1-40).[19]

Dizahab: This word in the Hebrew means "an abundance of gold," and may refer to both the "abundance of gold" the Israelites brought to the wilderness from the Egyptians (Exodus 12:35) and their having used some of it to make the golden calf and sin against God (Exodus 32).[20]

This is fascinating to consider, right? This is far more than a seemingly unfamiliar list of names to be skimmed over by our Western eyes.

Regardless of the reason for their specific mention–whether veiled rebuke or to otherwise help paint this particular space opposite others–the Israelites hearing these names mentioned would have points of reference to their story. They would better understand the history of these spaces, and they would find their inclusion helpful.

Moving to the parenthetical in verse 2, why do you think Moses includes this?

How long does this verse say it typically takes to travel from Horeb to Kadesh Barnea by the Mount Seir road?

---

[17] Scherman, Rabbi Nosson and Rabbi Meir Zlotovitz. The Stone Edition: The Chumash, 939.
[18] Ibid.
[19] Ibid.
[20] Ibid.

And, in verse 3, what timeframe does the author offer as the beginning of Moses' speeches to Israel? The _____ day of the _____ month of the _____ year.

This timing/calendar is in reference to their having left Egypt.[21]

Given the above timeline references, how much longer did Israel's travel take them?

Is this perhaps another (less) veiled rebuke?

As we will continue to learn, Israel had covered much ground, and little ground, in that amount of time. They had recently seen military victories over Sihon and Og (we will look into these further next week) and were standing east of the Jordan in the territory of Moab, ready to hear from their leader Moses.

In verses 6-8, Moses reminded Israel of the words the Lord had spoken to them at Mount Horeb (Mount Sinai), when He called them to enter the Promised Land.

This narrative is all a remembrance of one shared in Numbers 10:13 when, on the 20th day of the 2nd month of the 2nd year, the Lord commanded them to follow Him. (You may notice this is not immediately after their deliverance from Egypt. Israel spent time encamped near Mount Horeb, building the tabernacle and its furnishings and learning the statutes and covenant commands from the Lord.)

What did the Lord say to Israel?
You have stayed _____ _____ at this mountain (v6).

It was time to move! It was time to "break camp and advance!" (verse 7).

Advance to where? Verse 7 tells us the hill country of the Amorites…the neighboring peoples in the Arabah…to the Negev…to the land of the Canaanites…and to Lebanon as far as the Euphrates. These are all people and places we may not readily recognize, depending on our familiarity with the Old Testament. We will learn about some of these in the texts to come, but for now we can simply know that these were foreboding enemies of Israel. And yet the Lord was

---

[21] It was common for ancient Near East cultures to relate their calendars to key events rather than a fixed-date calendar. *NIV Cultural Backgrounds Bible*, 293.

calling them to *purposefully go to* them and *trust* He would be with them.

And, perhaps recognizing their propensity for fear, the Lord God of Israel, Yahweh, backed up these orders with words of promise in verse 8.

> **"See, I have given you this land. Go in and take possession of the land the Lord swore he would give to your fathers—to Abraham, Isaac, and Jacob—and to their descendants after them." (v8)**

"Go in and take possession." This is verbiage we will see oft repeated throughout Deuteronomy. Here, Moses is reminding Israel of God's command issued at Mt. Horeb some 38 years earlier (Exodus 33:1-2). And he is reminding them of God's encouragement in that same moment.

God reminded them of His earlier covenant promise with Abraham (Gen 12:7, 15:18, 17:7-8), Isaac (Gen 26:4), and Jacob (28:13). He had promised to give them, as the nation of Israel and as descendants of each of these men, the land of Canaan. And now He was commanding them to "go in and take possession" of it. They needed only to trust that the Lord would keep His long-awaited promise.

REFLECTION

Why did Israel experience a delay? Take a moment to write what you know about Israel's history in the wilderness. (It's okay if you don't know much or perhaps anything about this. You can use this as a "baseline" answer to know where you started. We will begin covering this more in two days.)

What can we learn from Israel's delay? (Again, you may not have a point of reference yet; what might they have learned that we can apply to our lives? We will cover this later as well.)

How does this section of text, with its potential reminders of failures and delays, serve to encourage Israel before they enter the Promised Land? How does it serve to encourage us today?

What did God mean when He said the Israelites had stayed long enough at the mountain? Have you ever stayed somewhere "long enough?" How did you know it was time to "break camp and advance?"

Israel was called to go into the land the Lord had promised them, but to do so they had to face known enemies. How would the reminder of the covenant (promising land) given to Abraham, Isaac, and Jacob encourage Israel? What would this cause the Israelites to remember?

Theologian Matthew Henry has this to share in reflection on Deuteronomy 1:8: "When God commands us to go forward in our Christian course, he sets the heavenly Canaan before us for our encouragement."[22] May we each recognize that heavenly Canaan before us, encouraging us to go in and trust God to keep His promises!

---

[22] Henry, Matthew. *A Commentary on the Whole Bible: Volume 1, Genesis to Deuteronomy.* (Old Tappan, NJ: Fleming H Revell Company, 1883), 727.

DAY TWO

Appointment of Leaders/Delegation
(Deuteronomy 1:9-18)

Welcome back! Let's continue in the text.

~•~•~

Read Deuteronomy 1:9-18.

This text recalls a portion of Israel's history when a judicial system was put into place, for the present time and for their time in the Promised Land. You can read the original narrative in Exodus 18. Moses' father-in-law, Jethro, saw that Moses alone was hearing all of the peoples' cases all day long, and he challenged Moses to distribute the load.

Read Exodus 18:17-27.

Can you hear the concern in Jethro's pleas with Moses? He knew Moses' calling to be Israel's representative before God (v19), and to teach Israel God's decrees (v20).

Standing on the plain of Moab, Moses wanted to remind Israel of this important move in their history. We need not be disturbed that Moses doesn't mention Jethro's role in this delegation; the goal in this recollection is to remember the highlights of Israel's history, and the main thrust in this text is the way the Lord had established delegation of leadership in the new nation of Israel.

And, in this piece of Israel's history, Moses was careful to encourage them to recognize (once again) that the Lord had kept His promise (at least metaphorically) to increase Israel's numbers to be as numerous as the stars of heaven (Gen 15:5 among other places). It is because of His promise kept that they became too much for one man to carry alone. The Lord was not surprised by this and helped them implement a system.

In verse 15, Moses said he took leading men of Israel's tribes and appointed them to have authority over others. The camps of Israel were separated and organized by tribe. (There were twelve tribes which correlated to the sons of Jacob, except for Joseph who had two half-tribes named for two of his sons.) The overseeing of judgments would come from brothers within their own tribe.

How were the people distributed? What was the largest number of people for which one person was responsible? _____
_____

The judges were commanded to be impartial–to "not show partiality in judging" and to "hear both great and small alike" (v17). In this way, they would reflect the character of their God, who was impartial (Deuteronomy 10:17; Acts 10:34-35; 1 Peter 1:17).

They were to not be afraid of anyone in their judgment on God's behalf. And, if any case was too difficult, they could bring it to Moses, their mediator with God, for his help.

REFLECTION

How did Jethro's insight help Moses and ultimately the nation of Israel? Do you see this model in place anywhere in your life today (secular or church)?

What are the dangers of trying to carry too much? What are the benefits of sharing the load?

Have you ever had someone confront you with a challenge they can see in your life and offer a solution you may not have considered? How did you respond?

Leviticus 19:15 warns the Israelites to "not pervert justice" and to "not show partiality to the poor or favoritism to the great." How might one be tempted to show partiality to the poor or favoritism to the great? (Note: James 2 warns against favoritism within the church as well.)

Looking ahead: In 1:16, the judges were called to "hear" the disputes and judge fairly on God's behalf. This Hebrew word *sema* is used 93 times in the book of Deuteronomy, and for the first time here.[23] Throughout Deuteronomy, the people were called to hear (*sema*) the Lord, through His servant Moses, and reveal they had, indeed, heard by living changed lives of obedience and love. We will be tracing this call to *"hear"* and the way it affects the *"heart"* throughout this study.

---

[23] Wiersbe, Warren W. *The Bible Exposition Commentary Old Testament: The Pentateuch, Genesis-Deuteronomy*, 380.

DAY THREE

Spies Sent Out
(Deuteronomy 1:19-25)

Time to "hear" more from Moses.

~•~•~

Read Deuteronomy 1:19-25.

This seems encouraging, right? They set out for the hill country, like God commanded. They could "go up and take possession" of the land, as the Lord God had, through Moses, told them. They need not be afraid or discouraged. What could go wrong? Was this foreshadowing on Moses' part?

The Israelites asked Moses if they could send men ahead of Israel into the land to give them a report about the land, the towns, and the route they might take. Again, Moses thought this idea reasonable. And, as he had for the judicial system earlier, he delegated men from each tribe (twelve in all) to go.

And, according to this account in Deuteronomy, the spies returned with a good report. "It is a good land that the Lord our God is giving us." (v25)

Once again, we can read the original narrative in Numbers.

Read Numbers 13:1-27.

The spies were to assess both the land and its people over the course of 40 days, and to report back to Israel.[24] The land was good, as could be proved by the grapes that accompanied them on their return.

How many men were needed to carry the cluster of grapes back to Kadesh?

_____

---

[24] Doty, Brant Lee. *Bible Study Textbook Series: Numbers.* (Joplin, MO: College Press, 1978), 146.

Incredible, right?! Once again, they had proof before their eyes that their God could be trusted–the land was, indeed, good and flowing with milk and honey, and every good thing. They could hear (and see) for themselves that God was giving them good things.

Throughout this account, Israel had settled in Kadesh Barnea (that original 11-day destination from Horeb). This was an area in the wilderness of Paran (as originally referenced in Deut 1:1) that was often seen as a "home base" or "headquarters" of sorts for Israel throughout their wandering years–a place to which they would likely return often.[25] It was also synonymous with the "wilderness of Zin" seen throughout the Old Testament.[26] And, as its name means "holy place," it was important in the history of Israel's existence even after entering the land (it would eventually become the southern boundary marker of Judah).[27] This place will appear throughout our walk in Deuteronomy.

REFLECTION

Why did Moses tell the people not to be afraid or discouraged? (He didn't say this in the earlier recount.)

How did the people react? What did they determine to do? (Be careful not to read ahead in Numbers or Deuteronomy.)

---

[25] Oberst, Bruce. *Bible Study Textbook Series: Deuteronomy*, 28.
[26] Ibid, 29.
[27] *NIV Cultural Backgrounds Bible*, 293.

How might the clusters of grapes (requiring two men to carry them) especially encourage the Israelites after two years in the desert?

Have you experienced a glimpse of the goodness of a space the Lord was calling you to step into? What has that looked like? Or if you have not, can you think of something that would encourage you to take a risk of faith? Share.

We end today with an encouraging report from the spies, that the Promised Land is, indeed, good as the God of Israel has always proclaimed. We end today encouraged that the Lord keeps His promises and that His people can be assured of His goodness in the places He has called them.

DAY FOUR

Rebellion Against the Lord – Part I
(Deuteronomy 1:26-36)

Yesterday we were left with a "good report" about the new land.
Today, we will examine the "other side" of that report
and the consequences for Israel as a result.

Read Deuteronomy 1:26-36.

What has happened? Why are the people "unwilling to go up?" What has caused their "hearts to melt in fear" and to determine that the "Lord hates [them]" and that He sought to "deliver [them] into the hands of the Amorites to destroy [them]?"

There was another side to the spies' report in Numbers 13. Let's read it now.

Read Numbers 13:28-33.

Everything was changed by a conjunction, "but." "But the people who live there are powerful, and the cities are fortified and very large." Foreboding people and foreboding cities with foreboding armies.

The Anakites and the Nephilim were said to be giants and were certain to incite fear among men. But these were men who had seen the mighty hand of God work in mysterious ways to deliver them from Pharaoh and his army. Had they so easily and quickly forgotten this?

Only Caleb countered the fearful report with a statement rooted in faith. "We should go up and take possession of the land, for we can certainly do it" (v30).

But the other spies continued to issue their bad report–a report rooted in fear. And it was this fear that most undoubtedly distorted their view of their saving God!

What did the spies say they seemed like in their own eyes (and to the giants in the land)? (v33) _____

Read Numbers 14:1-4.

The people grumbled and declared they wished they had died in Egypt (similar to the question they asked in the space of Suph). They rebelled against the Lord and even sought to find a new leader in place of Moses!

This account in Deuteronomy does not go into all of the details of the Numbers account, as many of them would already be familiar, but points to Moses' attempt to encourage them in the faith. He attempted to counter the fear. He reassured them that the Lord would go before them (as He had in the past) and would fight for them (as He had in Egypt, where they had cried out for His help). He would carry them (as He had in the past) all the way to this place (Kadesh).

Fear is a mighty opponent, and Israel would not be able to overcome it at this moment. They ultimately would experience failure here at Kadesh because of their fear and unbelief.[28]

Moses reminded Israel that the Lord was angry when He heard them grumbling and rebelling against Him. Their punishment was great. No one from that generation would enter the Promised Land (except Caleb and, we will see later, Joshua).

One additional noteworthy detail in this portion of Deuteronomy is the reminder to Israel (then and now) that the trustworthy Lord had gone "ahead of [them]" all along their wanderings, in a "fire by night" and in a "cloud by day," to "show [them] the way [they] should go" (v32-33). They had experienced firsthand the trustworthy guidance of the Lord Himself, and yet they did not trust Him in this. They did not trust where He was leading them.

REFLECTION

How did the fearful report about the people in the land affect the nation of Israel? Have you experienced anything similar in a group where fear of "giants" or "seemingly insurmountable opponents" loomed? Share.

---

[28] Wright, Christopher J.H. *Understanding the Bible Commentary Series: Deuteronomy.* (Grand Rapids, MI: Baker Books, 1996), 30.

How did Caleb's report differ from the other spies? Why do you think he was able to boldly offer this report?

Have you ever allowed fear to keep you from trusting the Lord and obeying Him in something He has called you to do? Share.

How could you give yourself a different report, like Caleb offered, to walk in faith rather than fear?

How do we as Christians today experience the leading of the Lord? How do we allow Him to "show us the way we should go?" Explain.

Looking ahead: Eventually Israel would return to Kadesh before their ultimate entrance to the Promised Land. Scholar Gary Millar speaks a redeeming thought about this when he says, "The place of failure revisited becomes an important junction on the road to success."[29] We will surely see this to be true for Israel, eventually, and I pray we might see this to be true in our own lives.

---

[29] Millar, J. Gary. *Now Choose Life: Theology and ethics in Deuteronomy.* (Downers Grove, IL: InterVarsity Press, 1998), 71.

DAY FIVE

Rebellion Against the Lord – Part II
(Deuteronomy 1:37-46)

Continued remembrance of the struggle of Israel and of Moses.

~ • ~ • ~

Read Deuteronomy 1:37-46.

All of Israel would be excluded from entering the Promised Land. Now, Moses reminds Israel that he, too, was excluded, and that they had a role to play in that.

It's not clear if this is because they provoked him to anger or because they didn't follow his instruction to glorify God, but regardless, Moses was punished for his own failure alongside Israel.

The corresponding account can be found in Numbers 20.

Read Numbers 20:1-13.

What a story. Moses was called to give the grumbling people the water they cried for, but he did not follow God's instructions completely. He struck the rock twice, rather than speaking to it, and spoke to the people rather than speaking to the rock. He revealed his own lack of trust in the Lord, and before the people he was leading, and so he would suffer consequences for his actions (v12).

Interestingly, in Exodus 17:6, Moses had been called to strike a rock to bring water out for the people. Why would he be condemned for doing something similar here?

In Deuteronomy, the Lord commissioned Joshua (Moses' assistant and the only spy besides Caleb to give a good report) as the one who would lead Israel into the new land. And in this rebuke and commission, Moses asks Israel to remember that the Lord told them to turn around and set out for desert along the Red Sea route (v40).

Then, in Deuteronomy 1:41, we see Israel desperately seek to overcorrect out of guilt and remorse. The doubters reacted to the discipline of the Lord by determining to go up and fight, but they would do so without the blessing of the Lord, and, as we will read in Numbers 14, without the presence of the Lord (without the ark of the covenant or Moses accompanying them).

Read Numbers 14:39-45.

Interestingly, the Israelites decided to follow the Lord's original command, but it was too late. The Lord would not join them and would allow them to face defeat.

In fact, Deuteronomy 1:45 said the Lord would not listen to them in their weeping when they returned to Kadesh. He "paid no attention" to their cries. They had acted in disobedience and had angered Him.

REFLECTION

How might Israel have been responsible for Moses' disobedience with the call to bring water from the rock?

Does God's punishment of Moses seem harsh? Why would this warrant Moses being barred from entering the Promised Land?

Why did Israel decide to go to the hill country when God told them to set out toward the desert?

How have we acted like Israel, naively or pridefully overcorrecting our actions when we realize we have failed to follow the Lord's command? Have you experienced this? Share.

WEEK ONE NOTES

WEEK TWO

Remember: Wanderings & War... Moses Will Not Enter

CHAPTERS 2-3

Welcome back! I hope you have rested from our journey through chapter 1 last week! This week, as promised, we will be looking further into the defeats of King Sihon and King Og, two battles that encouraged Israel shortly before Moses' great Deuteronomy sermons. These would be the first of the battles to be won by this new generation "trained up in a wilderness" and reliant upon God.[30]

We will encounter some warrior language and some verses that may be uncomfortable, but my hope is that we will exit this week with a new understanding and appreciation of the way these texts point to a faithful, unchanging God whose merciful heart can be seen, even in war texts.

---

[30] Henry, *A Commentary on the Whole Bible, Volume 1: Genesis-Deuteronomy*, 734.

DAY ONE

Wanderings in the Wilderness
(Deuteronomy 2:1-23)

**Begin by reading Chapter 2 in its entirety.
Then focus on Deuteronomy 2:1-23.**

This portion of text summarized the wandering of Israel, as they made their way around the country of Seir (over 38 years), in one verse. We need only to look at the other books of the Pentateuch to see that much occurred over those 38 years. But Moses chose to move forward to their more recent history, in God's care for the "extended family" of Israel and His faithfulness to not only Israel but to their relatives.

Moses' words in verses 2 through 6 remind Israel about God's command to them regarding the descendants of Esau they would encounter (originally chronicled in Numbers 20:14-21). They were not to provoke them or fight with them. They would not receive any of their land–it was for Esau's descendants to have as their own. It's important to note that Esau was the brother of Jacob (the father of the tribes of Israel, and himself renamed Israel). These were "cousins" of sorts to Israel. This was family territory, and God would not give this land to Israel.

And, though they were "family," Israel would not receive food or drink without payment. Indeed, God commanded them to pay (with silver) for the food and water they would receive.[31]

There are two other similar commands for two other groups (more family members) they would encounter (verses 9 and 16-19). Lot (the nephew of Abraham, the original recipient of the covenant and land promise) had two sons, Moab and Ben-Ammi, and the Moabites and Ammonites were descendants of these sons. The Lord provided land for each of them and protected them from battle with Israel. Theologian Walter Brueggeman says these passages remind us that "not everything about land concerns war" in the Old Testament.[32] Our hearts may need this reminder as we continue through the Old Testament texts about war and conquest in the new land and in the coming kingdom.

---

[31] Silver was a preferred medium of payment in ancient Near East cultures, and something Israel would have received from Egypt. They would not have had much to offer for a bartering payment, so silver was their best option. *NIV Cultural Backgrounds Bible*, 296.

[32] Brueggeman, Walter. *Abingdon Old Testament Commentaries: Deuteronomy.* (Nashville, TN: Abingdon Press, 2001), 42.

Within this section, there are also parentheticals (verses 10-12 and 20-22) that reference area giants that were destroyed by the Lord on behalf of these nations. We don't want to miss these sections and dismiss them as unimportant or hurry past them. These were real people living in a real time and these nations were delivered from the threat of these giants.

Does it feel ironic that these nations were delivered from the threat of the giants and, as we learned last week, the threat of giants (and more specifically the fear of them) was the very thing that had kept Israel wandering all these years?!

Working our way back up in the text, in verse 7, just after Moses mentioned that Israel paid for their food and water, he reminded Israel that the Lord had blessed them and watched over their journey. The Lord had provided for their every need. They lacked nothing (this is something we will revisit in week 7/chapter 8). Moses took the opportunity to remind them of the Lord's constant care and provision.

Did he remind them of this in the original context so they wouldn't grumble about the need to pay for their food and drink?

Consider: how much had Israel paid for food and drink in their years in the wilderness? _____

Or did he remind them of God's perfect care of them in response to the call to forgo taking these lands?

Regardless, Israel would, once again, be reminded of God's constant and perfect care for them all along the way!

And, almost as if in contrast to the blessing, Moses also inserts verses 14 and 15 to remind Israel of the discipline they had received, and the exchange of one generation of fighting men for another.

This section, though not gaining any conquered ground for Israel, has much to say about Israel's heart and the Lord's care for them. And much of it can relate to us.

REFLECTION

What does the text say about the Lord's hand during those 38 years in the wilderness (v15)? How can we reconcile this with the previous reminder of God's blessing throughout the wilderness (v7)? How can God be One who brings blessing and care and yet also discipline?

Have you experienced the Lord's blessing in your life? How have you seen evidence of His watching over you and caring for your needs? Share.

Had you considered God's gift of land to other nations before? What does this reveal about the Lord and His care for nations besides Israel?

WEEK TWO – DAY TWO

DAY TWO

Defeat of King Sihon
(Deuteronomy 2:24-37)

Today we will move from texts that call Israel to avoid battle and forgo taking land, to walk through texts that will excite us for Israel and yet make us uncomfortable for her enemies.

Let's dive in!

~ • ~ • ~

Read Deuteronomy 2:24-37.

That was a lot! The Lord gave Israel success with Sihon, but it was not without difficulty. (Note: You may choose to read this narrative in its original context in Numbers 21:21–26. For time's sake, we will simply work through this text in Deuteronomy.)

In this text, Moses reminded the nation of Israel that the Lord had commanded them to set out across the Arnon Gorge. He told them ahead of time that He would give them Sihon and his land, but it would require them to "engage him in battle" (verse 24). And engage him in battle, they would!

They had already passed by the land of their extended family, but now they would begin to encounter nations the Lord was removing from their path.

The Lord would reveal Himself as their defender and would surely act to reveal His sovereignty and might, not only in the victory of the battle but in the steps that led them to the battlefield.

Israel asked for peaceful passage, but Sihon refused.

What reason does the text give for Sihon's refusal (v30)? _____

_____

What does this mean? How does the Lord harden a heart? How does this reconcile with the free will of a man?

This is a mystery. But we can see this phenomenon in other places throughout Scripture, most notably in Exodus (7:3; 9:12; 10:20, 27; 11:10; 14:4) when God is said to have hardened Pharaoh's heart more than once in preparation for the deliverance by and glory of God in Israel's rescue.

One Bible scholar, Bruce Oberst, says that this is a way God showed His power over a king.[33] He also asserts that this is "not an example of causing a good man to become lost;" it was engaging with "a godless/sinful king (like Pharaoh) and bending him to His glory and the advantage of His people."[34] We see evidence of that in the Exodus story and in this battle with Sihon and his troops.

How would God's hardening of Sihon's heart work for God's glory and the advantage of His people? _____

_____

_____

Within this text, we come across some of the language the Old Testament is more notorious for including. We come across "total-kill" language, where Israel is said to have "completely destroyed" the region of Sihon–men, women, and children, leaving no survivors (v34). We will unpack this concept in greater measure when we come to chapter 7 (week 6), but right now it's most important to understand the highlights most scholars agree upon with this language.

Most scholars understand "total kill" language to be, most often, used within the Old Testament in hyperbole (exaggeration).[35] This was common within ancient Near East war literature.[36] Certainly, the culture at the time would have understood this. That said, there are examples in Israel's history where the Lord called for literal destruction of her enemies, but this was not routine and in each of these "holy wars," the conflicts were initiated by God and not the people themselves.[37]

---

[33] Oberst, Bruce. *Bible Study Textbook Series: Deuteronomy,* 57.
[34] Ibid, 56.
[35] Webb, William J. and Gordon K. Oeste. *Bloody, Brutal, and Barbaric? Wrestling with Troubling War Texts.* (Downers Grove, IL: InterVarsity Press, 2019), 14.
[36] Ibid, 14.
[37] Duguid, Iain M, general editor. *Numbers: God's Presence in the Wilderness.* (Wheaton, IL: Crossway Books, 2006), 330, 331.

These are weighty considerations, especially to our modern, Western understanding, but they were Israel's reality and part of her story, and part of the Lord's working to bring her into the Promised Land and to bring her heart more wholly devoted to Himself.

REFLECTION

How have you previously understood the war/destruction passages within Scripture? Has your study thus far made you reconsider that understanding? (Don't worry, we will study this further in a few weeks, but this is a good time to consider where your heart and head are in this concept.)

Why might God ask for His followers to completely destroy a nation? What benefit would this serve?

Did you notice the statement God made in verse 25? "This very day I will begin to put the terror and fear of you on all the nations under heaven. They will hear reports of you and will tremble and be in anguish because of you." How might the Israelites be encouraged by this?

Building upon verse 25 and looking ahead to the Israelites' further conquests in the Promised Land, take a moment to read Joshua 2:1-24. How did this "beginning" of trembling and fear work to Israel's benefit (emphasis Joshua 2:9)? And in a small digression, but with eyes on the gospel, how did this also eventually work to Rahab's (and our) benefit (Matthew 1:5)?

DAY THREE

Defeat of King Og
(Deuteronomy 3:1-11)

The first successful battle was under Israel's belt.
This would have encouraged Israel, and their hearts and minds
that weren't used to war, and could have served as a
discouragement to neighboring tribes who
might consider engaging in battle.[38]

Today, we will take a look at a neighbor who decided to engage.

Read chapter 3 in its entirety. Then, focus on Deuteronomy 3:1-11.

Israel conquered another king in the land. Another victory under their belt. The Lord had "delivered [Og] into [their] hands" (v2). (Note: You can read this account in Numbers 21:32-35.)

Once again, Israel completely destroyed the kingdom of an enemy. This time, the city was described as "fortified with high walls" (v5) and King Og was described as a giant (one of the last of the Rephaites, verse 11). Does this sound familiar?

What did the spies say about the land they had scouted? _____

What were the cities like (see Num 13:28)? _____

What were the people like (see Num 13:31-33)? _____

Israel was facing the very type of circumstances they had feared—the very things that had caused them to rebel against the Lord (and so wander in the wilderness for an additional 38 years).

---

[38] Oberst, Bruce. *Bible Study Textbook Series: Deuteronomy*, 57.

Is this coincidence? Or is this the wisdom of a good God who seeks to build confidence in His people as they prepare to go into the land He has prepared for them?

Let's look at that interesting parenthetical about the bed of Og in verse 11. Why is this included? Even without the understanding of the cubit measurement, we can appreciate this must be an impressive size, especially since it follows the classification of Og as a Rephaite/giant. This must have been extraordinary.

Why is the location of the bed (at the time of the reading) important to the reader?

It was common to keep items that commemorated or recalled the victory of the Lord over an enemy, especially when that enemy was of an especially impressive strength (like the sword that slew Goliath, etc.).[39] By regularly repeating the narrative and seeing the preserved bed of Og, Israel would be able to better remember the Lord's victory against the greatest of foes; indeed, against a giant!

REFLECTION

Have you been called to battle a proverbial giant in your life? What battle plans and strategies have you employed?

---

[39] *NIV Cultural Backgrounds Bible*, 299.

Have you seen the Lord overcome/conquer a giant (i.e., a trial) for you? How can you commemorate that victory? Do you have anything to serve as a constant reminder for you? Share.

One scholar has asserted, "Dwarfs and giants are all alike to God. The grand point is to keep God Himself ever before our eyes, and then our difficulties vanish."[40] Do you agree with this quote? How have you experienced this? How does keeping God before your eyes help you? What does that look like in practice?

---

[40] Oberst, Bruce. *Bible Study Textbook Series: Deuteronomy*, 62.

DAY FOUR

Division of Land
(Deuteronomy 3:12-20)

Okay, the battles are over, for now anyway.
Now, we are ready to see the distribution of the land
begin for the tribes of Israel. Can you believe it?

Let's look into this new season for Israel.

~•~•~

Read Deuteronomy 3:12-20.

Even before Israel formally crossed the Jordan to enter Canaan, some of the land east of the Jordan was parceled out to the tribes.

Moses was careful to explain the boundary lines of each of the land allotments. Ancient Israel would be familiar with these landmarks and the Jewish nation over time would recognize these geographical markers as well. Once again, these were real people living in real places at a real point in time and this documentation serves to confirm that.

In verses 18-20, Moses reminded Israel that these tribes, though they had already received their land, and their families could stay and begin to settle there, would be called to have their "able-bodied men, armed for battle" cross over the Jordan to help the other tribes receive their land. In Numbers 32:17, these able-bodied men of these tribes declared they would comply with this command.

Why would God call these tribes to do this?

Does this seem remarkable to you?

This isn't necessarily "natural" for any one of us. These men could have easily chosen to rest in their new land, but they knew that wasn't what the Lord had demanded of them. No, He demanded they continue marching with Israel as they went in to take possession of the land. Rest would need to come later. They would obey the Lord and look out for, and so serve, the interests of their brothers.

Would this be a witness to their own nation? Would this be a witness to the nations around them?

REFLECTION

How would the help of the early land recipients encourage the hearts of the tribes still yet to cross the Jordan and face threatening enemies?

This command to be selfless was certainly not exclusive to these tribes of Israel. As Christians, we have a similar command in the New Testament texts. Read Philippians 2:3-11. What are we commanded to do in this text?

How are we doing as a people and a "family" of God in living out this others-focused call in our lives? Do we step out of our places of rest and step into battle to help others find theirs? What may keep us from doing this?

How can you seek to serve others with great intentionality going forward?

DAY FIVE

Moses Forbidden to Cross the Jordan
(Deuteronomy 3:21-29)

Today we get a further glimpse into the heart of Moses, as he recalls the commission and encouragement for Joshua, as he recalls drawing near to the Lord in prayer (and pleading his case), and as he prepares for his long-awaited vision from atop Mount Pisgah.

Read Deuteronomy 3:21-29.

This isn't the first time we've been reminded of Moses' having been forbidden to cross the Jordan and enter the land. But in this text, we see some remarkable glimpses into Moses' character in the context of that reality.

First, even as Moses was fully aware he would not be entering the land he was called to lead Israel to enter, he took care to speak directly to Joshua and encourage his heart. He demonstrated the heart of a mentor. His charge to Joshua repeated the words so familiar to Moses' lips, "Do not be afraid!" He tells Joshua, "You've seen God destroy these enemy kingdoms. He will continue to do this against enemies in the new land!" (paraphrase mine). Joshua could be certain the Lord would continue to fight for him and for the nation of Israel. And Moses wanted to be certain Joshua did not forget.

The text then reveals to us the prayer of Moses, as he praised God for His goodness and pleaded with Him for mercy. And, in this, Moses demonstrated the heart of a humble intercessor. He also provided a model of prayer for a nation of worshipers.

> "For what god is there in heaven or on earth who can do the deeds and mighty works you do?" (v24).

In his prayer, Moses reminded himself, and the nation of Israel, of the mighty works and deeds of Yahweh. He recognized that his God was unlike any other gods.

What were some of God's deeds and mighty works Moses had seen in his lifetime? Take a moment to list the ones you know (so far in Deuteronomy or throughout the Pentateuch). _____
_____
_____
_____
_____
_____
_____
_____

It would seem pastoral genius to have this consideration at this point in the sermon, and this point in the text, as the next chapter will dive more deeply into the call to worship God alone and recognize Him as separate and above all other gods. What a gift we've all been given in the opportunity to reflect on this ahead of that chapter as well.

Finally, the text revealed God's answer to Moses, and, in that, Moses demonstrated the heart of a mature follower of God, able to speak objectively to those in his care. The Lord would not change His mind, but He would graciously allow Moses to see the land He was giving Israel from atop Mount Pisgah. He would also ensure Moses would commission Joshua, to encourage and strengthen him for the tasks ahead.

Read Numbers 27:12-23.

Here is the original account of Moses' commission of Joshua. He followed the command of the Lord and encouraged and strengthened Joshua in his leadership. What an example of humble obedience to the Lord and of humble service to Joshua.

Does anything stand out to you here?

REFLECTION

Read Psalm 71:16-19. How does this reflect the prayer (and life) of Moses? How can you apply this prayer to your own life?

Moses demonstrated exemplary devotion to God and leadership of those he was called to serve, even in the face of a seemingly unfavorable answer to prayer. Why is this remarkable? How have you conducted yourself in a season of seemingly unfavorable answers to your prayers?

In the work above, you were asked to consider the works and deeds of the Lord that Moses had seen and experienced. What are some works and deeds of the Lord you've seen and experienced in your lifetime? Make a list, or better yet write out your own prayer modeled on the above passage in Psalm 71 to praise the Lord for His goodness in your life.

WEEK TWO NOTES

WEEK THREE

Remember: Respond, Repent, Find Refuge

CHAPTER 4

This week, we will continue working through Moses' sermon and step into chapter 4. In this chapter, we will see Moses continue to move forward in his message to declare God's "decrees and laws" to Israel and to continue to emphasize the call to hear and wholeheartedly obey.

Moses will help Israel (and each of us) see the holiness of God, the nearness of God, and the mercy of God.

Let's get started!

DAY ONE

Hear, See, Obey
(Deuteronomy 4:1-8)

Let's see what Moses has for us today.

~•~•~

Read Deuteronomy 4:1-8.

Moses called Israel to *hear* the laws he was sharing with them. Did your ears perk up as you read this? I hope so! As we mentioned earlier, the call to "hear" is a thread that runs throughout Deuteronomy, but, so far, we've just encountered it in relation to legal proceedings (1:16-17) and others hearing reports about Yahweh's deliverance and victory for Israel (2:25).

In this text, Israel was called to *hear* Moses' teaching (from the Lord). He called them to pause and pay special attention, to heed what he was telling them–not just in this chapter, but over the course of the rest of the sermons he would preach as they prepared to enter the Promised Land.

And, in this particular text, before the bulk of the sermon, he added a warning to his "usual" teaching.

What is the warning Moses gives Israel in verse 2? _____

_____

How might they add to or subtract from the commands they heard? Why would this be wrong? _____

_____

_____

A warning such as this was common in ancient Near Eastern treaty literature.[41] To add or subtract to a legal or covenant treaty (which this document was likened to–see introduction) would mar its perfection; and, in this case, in a covenant with God, it would presume to "usurp

---
[41] Walton, John H., general editor. *Zondervan Illustrated Bible Backgrounds Commentary, Vol 1: Genesis, Exodus, Leviticus, Numbers, Deuteronomy*, 442.

the place of God."⁴² This would be counter to the heartbeat of Deuteronomy (and the covenant) in proper worship and regard for the God of Israel alone, over and above any god of man's design.

This warning was not only issued from Moses (though it will be one more time, just prior to a long list of commands in Deuteronomy 12:32). It was, much later, issued by the Apostle John in Revelation 22:18-19, when he gave a similar warning to believers (with stated consequences of curse and removal from the tree of life) about adding or subtracting to the scroll. The Word of God should be handled with care, by the Israelites then and the church today.

For times' sake, we will revisit verses 3-4 on day three this week.

In the next section, Moses repeated himself again (repetition is the name of the game for Moses), as he reminded Israel that the commands were for their benefit in the Promised Land (verse 5). But, in this section, he built on that foundation and shared the greater benefit of the law and careful adherence to it.

What did Moses say their observance of the commands would show (v6)?
_____
_____

And to whom would it be shown? _____
_____

Wisdom is more than simply "intelligence." It is a mark of character and a "right use of knowledge" that is not the same as simply learning facts. And, as this passage reveals (here and in verse 8), this wisdom demonstrated in Israel's obedience would allow them to live out their role as the priesthood of Yahweh before the nations.⁴³ Other nations would come to know the God of Israel as wise and, indeed, real, simply by the witness of His people.

The nation would not only be considered great because of this wisdom and understanding. No, they would also be regarded as great because of the nearness of their God (verse 7).

The nearness of God is not just a reality of the New Testament; it has been a reality all along. Yahweh, the God of Israel, was "near at hand" and "ready to help Israel if they [cried] out for help."⁴⁴ What other nation was so great to have this access to God? This would have

---

[42] Oberst, Bruce. *Bible Study Textbook Series: Deuteronomy*, 72.
[43] Wright, Christopher J.H. *Understanding the Bible Commentary Series: Deuteronomy*, 47.
[44] Connoway, Izaak J. and Johannes Malherbe. "The Proximity of Yahweh in Deuteronomy: A study of Key Phrases and Contexts" *Conspectus: The Journal of the South African Theological Seminary,* Oct 30 2020, 68.

been a remarkable reality for those living in an ancient Near East culture, and it is certainly still remarkable for those of us today living in a modern Western culture.

The nearness of God could be seen in His commands for Israel. Indeed, the careful guard of the commands and the careful obedience to these commands would demonstrate the existence and presence of a real, wise, faithful, and near God.

REFLECTION

Moses told Israel that their obedience to God's law, and so their personal daily conduct, would be a witness (a declaration of God's existence and character) to other nations. What might stand out to them? How would these differences bring attention to their God's existence and character?

How does your daily conduct declare God's existence and character to others?

What are some ways we may (even unintentionally) add or subtract from God's Word? How can we guard against this?

How is God's "nearness" to His people unique? How does this truth encourage you?

How have you experienced the "nearness of God?" Have others around you recognized this to be true (like the nations around Israel did)? Share.

DAY TWO

Words from the Fire
(Deuteronomy 4:9-14)

Today we are going to experience the Lord speaking to Israel
out of a fire, as they came near to hear His commands.

~•~•~

Read Deuteronomy 4:9-14.

"Only be careful..." Moses called on Israel to not only remember God's commands, but to also remember the day they heard them declared by the Lord. Bible scholar John Goldingay asserts the word "remember" is the most frequent command in the Bible.[45] God's people were to always remember, and never forget, the ways and words of their God.

Another scholar, Gary Millar, speaks specifically to the "remember-ing" that is done in Deuteronomy 4:10. He says that in this verse and passage, "Moses is calling Israel to an act of corporate imaginative remembrance as insights of the past are brought to bear on the decision of the present and future."[46] Indeed, Moses was calling on Israel to recall that day at Mt. Horeb–to remember the things they saw and heard, and what they felt and where they stood–to strengthen Israel's resolve as they moved forward.

From where did the Lord speak to the people (v12)? _____

_____

Read Exodus 19:1-9; 16-25 (background context of the event remembered).

As they remembered that day...

Could they see the flames of the fire? Could they smell the smoke in their midst? Could they feel the shaking of the thunder? Could they hear the booming voice of the Lord? Could they recall His words?

---

[45] Goldingay, John. *Do We Need the New Testament? Letting the Old Testament Speak for Itself.* (Downers Grove, IL: InterVarsity Press, 2015), 176.
[46] Millar, J. Gary. *Now Choose Life: Theology and Ethics in Deuteronomy,* 72.

How would this remembrance strengthen their resolve to move forward into the land? _____
_____

Could they share this with their children so they could know, and so "remember," themselves?

In verse 9, Moses gave Israel that very charge (again, a recurring theme throughout Deuteronomy). Concern for the generations that followed was of great importance to ancient Israel. The Old Testament historical narratives that follow this book recount the blessings and curses that came with subsequent generations with respect to their following the Lord. I would add that we can look to our own generational spiritual trees to help us recognize our need to be similarly concerned for the coming generations as well. Theologian Warren Wiersbe says, "Israel was always one generation short of losing God's blessing, and so it is with the church today!"[47]

Israel remembered hearing the Lord give the Ten Commandments to Moses and to them. And Moses had been charged to remind them of all they had heard (again and again) before they parted ways.

We will hear these words repeated a number of times (even within this chapter), and in the chapters that follow. Moses wants to be certain that Israel hears, that Israel remembers, and that Israel follows God's ways.

REFLECTION

Israel was called to remember the mighty way they had experienced the presence and instruction of the Lord. Memories, particularly with details that appeal to our senses and experiences as milestone moments, are powerful to our understanding and our encouragement. Can you recall a memory that was especially powerful in walking forward in your faith? What are some of the details you remember? What words were spoken to you at that time?

---

[47] Wiersbe, Warren W. *The Bible Exposition Commentary Old Testament: The Pentateuch, Genesis-Deuteronomy*, 382.

The Lord had Israel assembled so they would hear His words and learn to revere Him (and then teach the same to their children). How have you been learning to revere the Lord? What does that look like? How do children around you (in your family or community) benefit from this?

Has the Lord ever caught your attention like He did in the narratives we read today? How might you have reacted to a "mighty fire" and "thundering voice of God?"

DAY THREE

Have No Idols
(Deuteronomy 4:15-24; 25-28)

Moses will pick up the pace on his sermon and challenge Israel in their worship and practice.

~•~•~

Read Deuteronomy 4:15-24.

Moses warned Israel not to create any type of form, image, or idol to represent their God. This was actually one of the Ten Commandments they had received at Mt. Horeb. They were forbidden from "fashioning any divine images."[48] Moses suggests that, because they did not see any form, they should not be enticed to give Him a form in their worship. The official word for this practice is "aniconism," which means there is an "absence of a physical image of a deity for use in religious worship."[49]

Israel was to be aniconic in its worship practice.[50] It was to worship without idols or images.

Why would this be important? Moses made a good case for this within the text.

What do the things listed in verses 16-19 all have in common? _____
_____
_____

These are all things that were created by the Creator God. Any one of them is an underrepresentation of God. Any one of them is an inadequate picture of the character of God. Any one of them is not worthy of our worship.

---

[48] Middlemas, Jill Anne,. "Aniconism and Deuteronomy 4-5." *The Bible Today*, 56 no 3, May-June 2018, 154.
[49] Ibid., 151.
[50] Berlin, Adele and Mark Zvi Brettler, editors. *The Jewish Study Bible, Second Edition.* (New York, NY: Oxford University Press USA, 2014), 352.

The ancient Near East religions had many visual representations of their gods. They worshiped the created things rather than the Creator. Israel must not follow in their ways.

In verse 20, Moses used an interesting metaphor– "the iron-smelting furnace" when referencing the deliverance the Lord had given them.

What would this mean? This term may represent "a symbol of oppression" (this seems to make sense, doesn't it?), but the *NIV Cultural Backgrounds Bible* suggests it is "a creative force," transforming one object into another.[51] Indeed, scholar John Walton applies the transformation interpretation to this verse, as well, as he relates that the iron-smelting furnace would have been used to melt iron ore to a malleable state that would allow it to be fashioned into a desired end-product.[52] He asserts this can be seen in the way "the Exodus experience transformed Israel into the covenant people of God."[53]

So, the same furnace that could metaphorically represent the intense oppression Israel suffered under Egypt's rule could also represent the very vehicle of their transformation–the tool by which they were made malleable and fashionable into the covenant, inheritance, people of God! That's a beautiful redemption.

After this beautiful reminder of God's deliverance, Moses took the opportunity to remind Israel, once again, that he would not join them in the new land. (This appears to be a theme for Moses as well; not in a self-pitying way, but in a matter-of-fact urgency, like a father pressing to remind his son he would not always be with him.)

Let's remember: Why would Moses not enter the Promised Land? _____

_____

_____

Again, like a father, Moses' sharing may be an "urging the Israelites to learn from his personal experience and history."[54] It may also be a paternal longing for "Israel to live, though he must die."[55] He longed for them to do differently–to remember and obey the commands of God. He longed for them to do better, just as many a parent longs for their child.

---

[51] *NIV Cultural Backgrounds Bible*, 300.
[52] Walton, John H. *The IVP Bible Background Commentary: Genesis-Deuteronomy.* (Downers Grove, IL: InterVarsity Press, 1997), 225.
[53] Ibid.
[54] Hamilton, Victor P. *Handbook on the Pentateuch.* (Grand Rapids, MI: Baker Book House, 1982), 398.
[55] Ibid.

WEEK THREE – DAY THREE

Do you hear the urgency building in Moses' speech? Just after he anticipates his death, he tells Israel to "be careful not to forget." He pleads his case for their obedience.

What reason does he offer for not making idols (v24)? _____

_____

"God is a consuming fire, a jealous God" (Deut 4:24). What does this mean? First, God as a consuming fire is one who consumes dross or unholy/unpure aspects of an entity (like a refining process) or one who consumes his enemies.[56] The God of Israel is certainly both of these things.

I suspect that aspect of God was not concerning or surprising to you. If you're like many Western-minded readers, you likely struggle more with the concept of God being jealous. While unusual for a god in the ancient Near East (the other gods would not have been as personally engaged with their worshipers), jealousy in the context of a covenant partner was not as foreign. The covenant relationship had many parallels to a marriage covenant relationship, and, as such, it was to be an "exclusive relationship," which would exclude the worship of other gods.[57] As in marriage, the "goal of the covenant was fidelity."[58] The God of Israel would not tolerate infidelity.

Further, as a holy God, Yahweh would be "zealous for honor" as God alone.[59] The one true God would not share His honor with anyone or anything else.

Read Deuteronomy 4:25-28.

Moses continued his warning with a glimpse into the punishment for their potential idolatry. In verse 26, he specifically says that if they participate in idolatry and evil in the eyes of the Lord that He would destroy them.

Remember that we skipped discussing verses 3-4 on day 1? We will look at those now.

Those verses say: "You saw with your own eyes what the Lord did at Baal Peor. The Lord your God destroyed from among you everyone who followed the Baal of Peor, but all of you who held fast to the Lord your God are still alive today." This references an incident that is documented in Numbers 25.

---

[56] Walton, John H., general editor. *Zondervan Illustrated Bible Backgrounds Commentary, Vol 1: Genesis, Exodus, Leviticus, Numbers, Deuteronomy*, 446.
[57] Ibid.
[58] Ibid.
[59] Hess, Richard S. *The Old Testament: A Historical, Theological, and Critical Introduction.* (Grand Rapids, MI: Baker Academic, 2016), 145.

Read Numbers 25:1-9.

God would not tolerate Israel's participation in idolatry and evil practices. Interestingly, this incident happened following a victory of God in which Balaam (who had been hired by the Moabite king to curse Israel) was unable to curse Israel and instead declared blessing on Israel. After this, Israel appeared to "let down her guard" and succumbed to the "lust and gluttony" of their own desires to join the Moabite women in their idolatry.[60] And God called down destruction on Israel's participants as a result.

Warren Wiersbe wisely considers, "What the enemy couldn't accomplish with curses and fighting, he accomplished with compromise and friendship."[61] Indeed, that would appear to be the case.

Moses wanted to be sure they remembered this failure and the destruction it wrought. They would need to remember this danger when they entered the land. (We will want to remember this, too, when we get to chapter 7.)

Unfortunately, this isn't the only reminder Israel would need. They would revisit this struggle throughout their history. And they would see the declaration of verses 27-28 come to fruition in various exiles and scatterings because of their disobedience. The Lord is a holy and jealous God who will discipline His people.

REFLECTION

Have you experienced a great hardship/difficulty and found yourself transformed as a result? Share.

---

[60] Doty, Brant Lee. *Bible Study Textbook Series: Numbers*, 275.
[61] Wiersbe, Warren W. *The Bible Exposition Commentary Old Testament: The Pentateuch, Genesis-Deuteronomy*, 381.

How does that experience and the truths in God's Word about His refining and ability to use difficult times for His glory (and our good) bring you hope?

How can God's jealousy be regarded as good? How does it differ from man's jealousy?

James 4:4 tells us not to become friendly with the world—that doing so is an infidelity to God. We saw an example of this in our reading in Numbers this week. How have you experienced something similar (or have you)? How can you protect yourself from becoming "too friendly" with the world? How does a Christian who is called to preach the good news to the world practice and obey both commands?

DAY FOUR

Repentance & Rescue
(Deuteronomy 4:29-40)

Idolatry, trickery, destruction, and exile. Yesterday was heavy.
Let's see if Moses has some hope for us today.

~•~•~

Read Deuteronomy 4:29-31.

What (or whom) will Israel find if they seek God after their fling with idolatry? _____

This is the mercy of God! We can see it here, in the pages of the Old Testament! Gospel hope is found within the pages of Deuteronomy! Israel could return to God and find Him. And God would respond with mercy and grace. He would not abandon or destroy them, nor forget His covenant.

John Walton says that this passage reveals that "even a betrayed husband and covenant partner could be reconciled."[62] Indeed, a heart of repentance (seeking to turn away from sin and back toward God) would be met with forgiveness and mercy and restoration and grace. This is similar to the hope we have in Jesus Christ today! Hallelujah!

Let's see if the encouragement continues.

Read Deuteronomy 4:32-40.

Moses made a case for the goodness of God. Who is like the Creator God? Who has heard the voice of God speaking out of fire and lived? What other God has made and cared for a nation for Himself?

---

[62] Walton, John H., general editor. *Zondervan Illustrated Bible Backgrounds Commentary, Vol 1: Genesis, Exodus, Leviticus, Numbers, Deuteronomy*, 446.

Why was Israel shown these things (v35)? _____

_____

_____

The *Chumash* (a rabbinical commentary on the Hebrew Bible) interprets this verse with this statement, "God allowed you the privilege of experiencing all these wondrous phenomena so that you would meditate upon them and draw the unshakable conclusion that only [Yahweh] is God."[63] Moses was determined to ensure Israel recognized the awesome might, power, and grace of their God as well.

Let's consider some of that might, power, and grace in Israel's story.

Read Exodus 13:17-22 & 14:1-31.

Take time to list God's might, power, and grace towards Israel. _____

_____

_____

_____

_____

_____

_____

_____

_____

_____

_____

This is the climax of the Exodus story–the main display of saving activity as Moses led Israel out of Egypt and Pharaoh and his army pursued. This portion of Israel's story came after many testings and signs (plagues) against Egypt and preceded many further testings for Israel.

This deliverance text revealed the mighty hand and outstretched arm of the Lord (as referenced in Deut 4:34). These were among the great and awesome deeds the Lord God did for them, before their very eyes! These were among the many graces Israel would receive!

---

[63] Scherman, Rabbi Nosson and Rabbi Meir Zlotovitz. *The Stone Edition: The Chumash*, 965.

REFLECTION

Were you surprised to find the picture of a merciful God in this Deuteronomy 4 text? How does this mercy and promise to not destroy the repentant person reconcile with the texts that call for destruction of those who do evil?

How does the reality that God is in heaven above *and* on earth below (Deut 4:39) give you comfort? (Or does it?) How can our God be in more than one place?

Read Psalm 86:5-13. Let the words of the psalmist and the words of Moses in today's text lead you to praise the great and awesome God we serve. Write a prayer of thanksgiving to God for the many ways you've seen Him reveal Himself unlike any other.

WEEK THREE – DAY FIVE

DAY FIVE

Cities of Refuge
(Deuteronomy 4:41-43)

Today we will cover just a few verses (literally three),
but it's my prayer that you will see much depth
and hope within these three brief sentences.

Let's get started.

Read Deuteronomy 4:41-43.

Who could flee to these cities (v42)? _____

The Lord set aside cities for sanctuary for those who "unintentionally killed" someone. This was woven into the plans for the land inheritance all along.

What might this look like in practice today?

We don't really have a point of reference in our own culture, so this will take a little bit of unpacking.

The cities of refuge were "cities within cities" overseen by Levites (who did not receive an inheritance of their own).[64] A person who unintentionally killed another could flee to these cities and be kept safe. See, ancient law allowed for an "avenger of blood" (male next of kin of the deceased) to pursue the killer to avenge their loved one's death.[65] If the accused killer was able to outrun the avenger, they could find safety and provision in the city of refuge.

These concepts may seem difficult for our Western hearts and minds, but they have a rich theological application.

---

[64] Doty, Brant Lee. *Bible Study Textbook Series: Numbers*, 371.
[65] Ibid, 371.

The existence of cities of refuge (and the avenger of blood) actually points to "the inherent value of each individual life"[66] and "the awesome nature of divine justice."[67] The Lord did not condone murder, but He sought to protect the lives of those who unintentionally found themselves guilty and to protect the dignity and honor of those who died.

Another incredible aspect of the cities of refuge is that they were, in reality, quite inconvenient, especially economically.[68] Remarkably, though, as Brueggeman considers, "Israel committed to inconvenience that fostered life."[69] Israel was committed to caring for others in ways that mirrored their God's care for them, regardless of its economic sense or lack thereof.

Finally, the inclusion of these cities' names helps add credibility to the account, illustrate the intentional distribution of sanctuary, and, as they are all in the land inheritance east of the Jordan, demonstrate God's care for Israel even before they crossed the Jordan. The God of Israel–the same God we serve today–was and is a God of details.

REFLECTION

What would our society and justice system look like if we had cities of refuge today? Would they be a help or hindrance to the justice system? Would they serve as a witness to God?

---

[66] Lange, John Peter, Phillip Schaff, and Wilhelm Julius Schroeder. *A Commentary on the Holy Scriptures: Deuteronomy*, 85.
[67] Doty, Brant Lee. *Bible Study Textbook Series: Numbers*, 371.
[68] Brueggeman, Walter. *Abingdon Old Testament Commentaries: Deuteronomy*, 59.
[69] Ibid.

How would relatives of persons killed accidentally be called to trust the Lord in these situations? How does this differ from our judicial system in our democratic state?

What pressures or difficulties might the refugee face within the city of refuge? How would the residents of that city be called to trust the Lord themselves as they care for this person?

P.S. For the grammatically inclined: Did you notice the change from first-person pronouns to a third-person reference to "Moses" in this portion of the text? This doesn't have to trouble us, as scholars have suggested this can be easily explained by an editorial appendix (still in the style of Moses and his teaching within the book) that was added to this portion of the text at a later date[70] or as a parenthetical offered by Moses himself (which he does in other portions of the book as well).[71] Either way, we can trust this is still the inspired word of God relating the narrative of Israel and Moses' instruction to them.

---

[70] Berlin, Adele and Mark Zvi Brettler, *The Jewish Study Bible, Second Edition*, 355.
[71] Oberst, Bruce. *Bible Study Textbook Series: Deuteronomy*, 84.

WEEK THREE NOTES

WEEK FOUR

Remember: Take These Words to Heart

CHAPTERS 4:44-49 & 5

All the text preceding this has been moving and looking toward this week's material–the commands of the Lord. This will not be the last time we work toward the commands of the Lord (the core of Deuteronomy is full of more commands in chapters 12-26, which we will tackle in the next volume of this study), but this is a foundational piece to all other commands Moses and the Israelites will consider and a foundational piece to our lives as followers of Christ.

Let's see what these words (also known as the Ten Words) have to say.

DAY ONE

Introduction to the Law
(Deuteronomy 4:44-49; 5:1-3)

This week we see one of those spots where the chapter divisions don't always ideally align with the overall context of the text. We will read the last portion of chapter 4 and then into chapter 5.

~ • ~ • ~

Read Deuteronomy 4:44-49; 5:1-3.

The conclusion of chapter 4 provides the introduction to chapter 5 (and actually to the entirety of the remaining chapters). This text reminds us of the setting for all of these sermons and reminders. Moses and the nation of Israel were in the valley of Beth Peor, the land of Sihon and the land of Og, with boundaries that are clearly defined and mirror those given in the opening of the book in chapter 1.

While they were encamped in this place, Moses summoned all Israel and began his declarations of the law.

As he has throughout the book, Moses reminded Israel of God's covenant with them at Horeb, but here he especially emphasized that the covenant was with their generation as much as it was with the prior (v2-3). He was not negating the importance of the previous generation's having received the covenant. Rather, he was "appealing that his contemporaries fully appropriate the earlier covenant for themselves."[72] This was not just for a previous generation. He will continue to make this point in this chapter (as he has throughout Deuteronomy) as he engages Israel in the story of their deliverance. Scholar Brad Kelle contends that Moses' "fresh telling of the story of Yahweh's deliverance and giving of the covenant and law" serves to "pull the new generation into God's story as if they'd been there all along."[73]

---

[72] Hamilton, Victor P. *Handbook on the Pentateuch.* (Grand Rapids, MI: Baker Book House, 1982), 404.
[73] Kelle, Brad E. *Telling the Old Testament Story: God's Mission and God's People.* (Nashville, TN: Abingdon Press, 2017), 106.

Why would this generation need to embrace this covenant for themselves?

Understanding their own identity as covenant recipients, chosen by God, would be key to strengthening them for the battles that remained. It is key for us as well!

Before we proceed with the specific laws that were recited before Israel that day, let's pause to consider what "law" meant to ancient Israel, to be sure we are looking at it with proper perspective.

What do you think of when you think of the word "law"?

For many of us today, the word "law" can carry connotations of restriction, punishment, and even harsh authority. It can conjure up images of legalism with impossible expectations and outright oppressive conditions where freedom seems limited or nonexistent. This would not have been the view of the ancient Israelite.

The "law" for the Israelite was simply a body of "God's expectations for the moral and spiritual conduct of Israel."[74] This doesn't really surprise us, does it?

What may surprise us is the fact that the ancient Israelites actually felt "celebration and gratitude for God's law;" they knew it to bring "benefit" to their lives.[75] The "law of God" revealed a "way of life" that Israel engaged in "as a response of love and gratitude to God."[76]

Is this how we view our laws? Is this how we view the commands of God?

Interestingly, though we have already seen many instances of grumbling and complaining by the Israelites throughout their wilderness wandering, a closer look at those complaints reveals that the Israelites are never heard complaining about the "burdensomeness of the law."[77] They might complain about their circumstances and their fear for their lives, but they would not complain about the justice or burden of the law God had given them.

This is remarkable!

---

[74] Ryken, Leland, James C. Wilhoit, and Tremper Longman, III. *Dictionary of Biblical Imagery*. (Downers Grove, IL: InterVarsity Press, 1998), 489.
[75] Ibid., 490.
[76] Motyer, J.A. *The Message of Exodus: The Days of our Pilgrimage*. (Downers Grove, IL: InterVarsity Press, 2005), 213.
[77] Hill, Andrew E. and John A. Walton, editors. *A Survey of the Old Testament, Third Edition*, 175.

As we prepare to walk through the Ten Commandments, also called the Decalogue (Ten Words), this week we will also want to keep in mind these further truths about the law. This will make every difference in our application of each of these laws to our lives today.

First, all of the laws within the Pentateuch (the first five books of the Bible) are said to reveal the character of Yahweh, something which has not changed.[78] The revelation of God's character to the ancient Israelite still benefits us, that we might know the character of God today.

Second, the Decalogue was understood to "give a framework for the essential characteristics and values of a community."[79] As a part of a community of believers (the church), and a community of society, we can all benefit from living by these laws as we seek to reflect the character of God.

Finally, especially as those living under the new covenant, and perhaps concerned about potential legalism in a zeal for the law, we will want to remember an important truth about the law that many of us may have misunderstood in the past. Similar to the earlier revelation that Israel viewed God's law with gratitude, it is important for us to realize what they understood: "we do not obey to win God's grace" but "we obey because we have received His grace."[80]

(Does this statement about ancient Israel surprise you? Israel's zeal for righteousness may have skewed our understanding of their view in this. At the heart of the matter, we are not as different as we may have considered ourselves to be!)

REFLECTION

We considered why Israel needed to personalize the covenant for themselves. Have you done similar with the promises of God in Christ? How has that impacted your walk with God? Share.

---

[78] Walton, John H. and D. Brent Sandy. *The Lost World of Scripture: Ancient Literary Culture and Biblical Authority*. (Downers Grove, IL: InterVarsity Press, 2013), 221.

[79] Alexander, T. Desmond and David W. Baker, editors. *The Dictionary of the Old Testament: Pentateuch*. (Downers Grove, IL: InterVarsity Press, 2003), 178.

[80] Richter, Sandra L. *The Epic of Eden: A Christian Entry into the Old Testament*, 85.

Have you received a "call to action" or "call to order" through historical storytelling similar to the Israelites? (e.g., employee orientations, ministry/committee meetings, family reunions, etc.) How did you better understand the importance of your specific role differently as a result?

Had you considered the benefits of the law before today? How have you benefited from the law? Societal? Biblical? How do you see characteristics of God in each of these laws? (even the secular laws may point to truths of God in some fashion)

Before we dig into the Ten Commandments, can you list them (without peeking) here? See what you can recall before we study them. I'm confident you will know them far more readily by the end of this week's work.

DAY TWO

Words of Instruction: A Closer Look – Part I
(Deuteronomy 5:4-10)

Now that we have a better understanding of how the Israelites would have viewed and received these laws, we're ready to begin to consider each command within the text. Today, we will start with the first two commands.

~ • ~ • ~

Read Deuteronomy 5:4-10.

In the opening of this text, Moses reminded Israel of the Lord's first deliverance of the law. We already explored one segment of that text, but today's text adds a dimension we did not read earlier. Moses referenced their having been afraid of the fire and not going up the mountain (v5). For context, let's jump to another section of the Pentateuch.

Read Exodus 20:18-21.

Interestingly, even though Israel was afraid, and sought to have Moses as their mediator to hear from God on their behalf, we know (from our earlier text and the continued references to Israel hearing God speak to them out of the fire) that God ensured Israel would also hear His voice with their own ears; they would receive the law through both mediated and direct divine speech from their God.[81] The Israelites could be sure they had heard from the Lord.

Let's head back to the text in Deuteronomy 5.

In verse 6, the God of Israel reminds them of His identity and character. Theologian Richard Hess calls this a "formula of self-identification," wherein God identified Himself as the One who had "claimed a people for himself on the basis of a miraculous event," having redeemed Israel from slavery to freedom.[82] His identity as their Lord and God, and the One who had redeemed

---

[81] Connoway, Izaak J. and Johannes Malherbe. "The Proximity of Yahweh in Deuteronomy: A Study of Key Phrases and Contexts," 71.

[82] Hess, Richard S. *The Old Testament: A Historical, Theological, and Critical Introduction*, 143.

them, would carry authority and allegiance.

Another important consideration in the sharing of the Decalogue—The Ten Commandments—is the use of the singular pronoun, "you." Scholars note this "stresses God's directly addressing each former slave as human beings."[83] This would stand out in a culture and nation that otherwise heavily focused on community. This also stands in contrast to the "plural you" used in the later commandments in Deuteronomy chapters 11 and following.

Let's consider the commandments themselves.

First Commandment: _____ (v7)

Theologian John Walton calls this the "central requirement of the covenant;" a "total allegiance of covenant love to Yahweh alone."[84] All of the commands in the covenant hinged upon obedience to this command. We've considered the reality of this command in our study of chapter 4, and we will consider this further when we study the text of chapter 6.

How might "having no other gods before Yahweh" benefit Israel and affect their ability to keep all the other commands? _____
_____
_____

The first four commands of the Decalogue were tied to Israel's relationship to God personally. Israel's proper regard and love for God was closely tied to love of neighbor (as a reflection of the God of Israel).[85] Having no other gods would keep Israel committed to worshiping and reflecting the character of the one true God.

Second Commandment: _____
_____ (v8)

We spent an extensive time discussing this last week, and, as we saw, the Lord holds Israel to a high standard in this.

This command may feel less applicable to us in our modern society. We don't often actively create or purchase statues or other icons to set before us so we may pay homage or bow down in

---

[83] Berlin, Adele and Mark Zvi Brettler, *The Jewish Study Bible*, 355.
[84] Walton, John H., general editor. *Zondervan Illustrated Bible Backgrounds Commentary, Vol 1: Genesis, Exodus, Leviticus, Numbers, Deuteronomy*, 444.
[85] Berlin, Adele and Mark Zvi Brettler, *The Jewish Study Bible*, 355.

worship before them. (Is that what you have pictured?)

That may be true, but we have certainly been guilty of finding our hearts trusting in things besides our God to save us, provide for us, care for us, or give us identity and purpose. We can find ourselves looking to the "ways of this world" for comfort, satisfaction, and rest, allowing those things to push our allegiance and worship of God to the side.

> **How can we identify a potential idol in our life? What, if you were to lose it today, would cause you great devastation and insecurity?** _____
> _____
> _____

Your answer to the above question may not in and of itself be an idol, but it is good to pay attention to the things–people, items, titles, statuses, or circumstances–that come to mind when we consider a question such as this. While God certainly cares about our relationships and our needs, He has also asked for our wholehearted allegiance to Him over and above all others.

REFLECTION

> **How might Israel have been tempted to have other gods before (or in addition to) Yahweh? Why would it be important for Moses to remind them of this command for wholehearted worship of Yahweh alone?**

Have you found yourself making an image for yourself and your worship? How is this different from having items or images that remind us of God's Word, presence, or activity? When could this become worship? Explain.

What about placing your "trust" in things and/or people other than God? Have you found yourself doing this? (Does your answer to the question of devastation help you consider this?) Explain.

In response to reading verses 9 & 10, do you tend to focus on God's promised punishment or blessing? Why do you think that is? Do you focus more on God's punitive nature or merciful nature? (Note: It's important to note that the punishment to the third and fourth generations was a reference to the generations a person would see during their lifetime. It was actually a mercy that the consequence and its effects would only last a few generations, while the blessing could last across many generations.)

DAY THREE

Words of Instruction: A Closer Look – Part II
(Deuteronomy 5:11-15)

This week we continue looking at the Ten Commandments
with respect to our relationship with God.

~•~•~

Read Deuteronomy 5:11-15.

Third Commandment: _____
_____ (v11)

You may have learned this as "you shall not take the Lord's name in vain." How did you understand this command in that context? I learned that it was to avoid using the Lord's name in a curse against Him (as in blaming Him for an unfortunate state of events) or to avoid using unsavory words as a whole. I imagine you may have a similar understanding of this command.

Interestingly, it is far more than that. It is about showing honor to God's name, with our lips and our lives. The personal name of someone in the ancient Near East revealed the "character and identity" of that person (in this case a deity).[86] To misuse someone's name would be to bring disrespect or dishonor to their character and identity.

When we recognize that the divine name of God is sacred, the weight of this dishonor is far greater. To take God's name in vain, or to misuse it may include slander, insult, deriding jest, or any activity that detracts from God's glory, all of which constitute a biblical term called blasphemy.[87] It would include a blatant misrepresentation of God and His character. Indeed, Gesenius' lexicon interprets this as meaning it is wrong to "utter the name of Jehovah upon a falsehood."[88] Any of these misuses of God's name attempts to minimize God's glory, whether intentionally or unintentionally.

---

[86] Alexander, T. Desmond and David W. Baker, editors. *The Dictionary of the Old Testament: Pentateuch*, 176.
[87] Holsteen, Nathan D. and Michael J. Svigel. *Exploring Christian Theology*. (Minneapolis, MN: Bethany House Publishers, 2014), 142.
[88] Oberst, Bruce. *Bible Study Textbook Series: Deuteronomy*, 93.

In keeping with the above, what about ascribing something to God that may not be wholly true? "The Lord told me to…" or "Surely God wouldn't want me to be unhappy." Would this also be misappropriating His name?

Ancient Israelites were actually known to have such high regard for this commandment that they devised different names/ways to refer to God's name without saying the divine name (Yahweh) aloud, by substituting the word Adonai when reading from the biblical text. Is this the heart of this command? Are we called to act in a similar manner?

In the New Testament, Jesus reminds us that we will be held accountable for every careless word we utter (Matthew 12:36). It would seem all the more so for the ways we misuse the holy name of God.

Fourth Commandment: _____
_____ **(v12)**

In Genesis, the Sabbath was understood as a remembrance of God's rest from His finished work as Creator (Genesis 2:2-3). In Deuteronomy, the Sabbath was understood as a remembrance of the Exodus and the rest for Israel as they trusted in God.

What have you considered the proper application of this commandment? Have you, like me, understood this to mean it is important for you to worship God in His house (the local church) every week, and to rest from work, and maybe take a nap, on that day?

The Sabbath was actually "a celebration of life outside of productivity."[89] It was to be an "act of resistance" where the key aim was not necessarily "worship" but "rest."[90] This would have been especially important, and a stark contrast of practice, for a nation of peoples who had not been accustomed to rest (after years of slavery).[91] Israel would reveal her trust in God's provision and care by honoring and keeping the Sabbath, resting from her work one day each week.

Israel had a unique opportunity to experience the importance of the Sabbath during their wilderness wandering, when the provision of food from heaven (manna) followed the rhythm of the Sabbath. (The manna did not fall on the Sabbath, so they could not work to collect it; they

---

[89] Brueggeman, Walter. *Abingdon Old Testament Commentaries: Deuteronomy*, 71.
[90] Ibid., 73.
[91] Martin, Oren R. *Bound for the Promised Land: The Land Promised in God's Redemptive Plan.* (Downers Grove, IL: InterVarsity Press, 2015), 85.

were to gather a double portion the day prior, by which God provided plenty to meet Israel's needs.) They lived this reality in very practical ways for 40 years, and yet they needed to be reminded of the importance of keeping the Sabbath in complete trust and rest in their Lord.

How much more so would our modern, Western, technologically advanced and highly connected society benefit from the rhythm of rest found within a keeping of Sabbath?

REFLECTION

Today, we considered what constituted the misuse of God's name. Was anything new to you? How can you guard your lips (and heart) from maligning God's name? How should you react when you are with others who disregard the name of the Lord?

How has this week's study changed your understanding of Sabbath? Or has it? Have you given serious attention to "keeping Sabbath" in the past, apart from simply attending church regularly? If so, what has been your practice? What has worked, and what has not?

Is it hard for you to "cease" being productive for a day? What practical steps can you take to help you grow in this area? How can you purposefully approach the Sabbath as a celebration of life outside productivity?

What is God's desire for the keeping of Sabbath? Are we to refuse to do *any* work that may be required on a Sabbath day? How can we know what is resting in God and what is striving to be productive? (Hint: Jesus had some thoughts on this He shared with the religious leaders of His day. Reflect on His practices–healing on the Sabbath, etc., as you consider your own approach to Sabbath keeping. This is about the *heart* of the law, not the legalistic keeping of the law, to the detriment of our neighbor.)

DAY FOUR

Words of Instruction: A Closer Look – Part III
(Deuteronomy 5:16-22)

In this section, we move from the commandments about our conduct towards God, and we consider our obligations to God with regards to our relationships with others.

~•~•~

Read Deuteronomy 5:16-22.

Fifth Commandment: _____
_____ (v16)

This text has often been considered of great importance for children to learn in their formative years, but in its original context, it was actually a special kindness toward the care and honor of aging parents by their adult children. In ancient Near East culture, the elderly were often neglected or even abused by the younger generation.[92] This care for the older generation revealed the heart of Israel's God. It revealed that not one person was expendable; it honored and protected the life of those deemed "unimportant, unproductive, or burdensome."[93] This commandment is far more than simply a child obeying his or her parents.

Before we move to the next commandment, did you notice the blessing and benefit that is added to this command? It says to honor your father and mother, "so that you may live long and that it may go well with you in the land the Lord your God is giving you." This was the first command to offer a promise. And this promise "that it may go well with you" would point to God's intention to prosper His people in the land of Canaan.[94] (We will continue to see this as a reminded benefit of obedience to God's law.)

---

[92] Wiersbe, Warren W. *The Bible Exposition Commentary Old Testament: The Pentateuch, Genesis-Deuteronomy*, 386.
[93] Alexander, T. Desmond and David W. Baker, editors. *The Dictionary of the Old Testament: Pentateuch.* (Downers Grove, IL: InterVarsity Press, 2003), 177.
[94] Smith, Richard L. "Such a Heart as This: The Intellectual Implications of Deuteronomy 5:29" *Evangelical Review of Theology*, vol 46, iss 1, Feb 2022, 28.

WEEK FOUR – DAY FOUR

Sixth Commandment: _____ **(v17)**

One scholar suggests this prohibition of killing may "seem ironic given the amount of violence contained within the Old Testament."[95] This is a fair assessment to consider, particularly within this book which celebrates the anticipated great destruction victories of God. That said, this command against killing does not include the killing involved in war or capital punishment.[96]

In the New Testament, Jesus took this commandment further to consider not only the action of murder but the hatred (and, so disregard or disdain for life) of another (Matthew 5:21-22). The spirit of this law is a matter of the heart.

Seventh Commandment: _____ **(v18)**

This law "seeks to preserve family order and so the larger order of society."[97] The marriage affected far more than just one's relationship with their spouse or relationship with the people in their family/household. Fidelity to the covenant of marriage had the potential to affect all spheres of a person's life, and as such it must be protected and diligently pursued. (We covered some of this fidelity focus earlier.)

Eighth Commandment: _____ **(v19)**

This had application in realms far greater than just material property. Some examples of things God's people were not to steal included: property, a person's good name (slander), status or standing (such as cheating on an examination or government paperwork which may have application in the ninth commandment as well), or other people (slaves/workers, kidnapping).[98] Have you considered any of these as types of theft before? Our God has provided all we need. Will we trust Him and resist the temptation to take what is not ours?

Ninth Commandment: _____
_____ **(v20)**

---

[95] Alexander, T. Desmond and David W. Baker, editors. *The Dictionary of the Old Testament: Pentateuch.* (Downers Grove, IL: InterVarsity Press, 2003), 177.
[96] Hess, Richard S. *The Old Testament: A Historical, Theological, and Critical Introduction,* 147.
[97] Ibid., 148.
[98] Wiersbe, Warren W. *The Bible Exposition Commentary Old Testament: The Pentateuch, Genesis-Deuteronomy,* 386.

In other words, Israel was not to lie. Wiersbe says, "truth is the cement that holds society together."[99] Indeed, without it, there cannot be order or harmonious relationships. We must always "deal truthfully with our neighbor" and "about our neighbor."[100] As people of a God of truth, Israel was called to reflect that truth, and we are called to do the same.

Tenth Commandment: _____
_____
_____ (v21)

What does it mean to covet? Look up the definition. _____
_____
_____

God warned Israel against yearning or desiring things which did not belong to them. This command contains a list of specific items (people and things) Israel should not covet. Interestingly, when placed against the list of these commandments in Exodus 20, this list is in a reversed order (in the Exodus account the property is listed before persons). Theologian Richard Hess explains this difference with regards to the needs of the nation in those distinctly different points in time. He asserts that the Exodus proclamation (immediately upon leaving Egypt) focused on property while the Deuteronomy proclamation (just prior to entering the Promised Land, with promised gifts of property and abundance) focused on the covenant relationships and moral bonds within one's family as priority.[101] This seems to correlate with the wife being listed before the property in Deuteronomy.

Another notable distinction the listing of the wife ahead of the property in this list seems to make is the fact that "the law does not regard women as merely one commodity among others."[102] Interestingly, theologians consider this "consistent with Deuteronomy's general view of women."[103] We can tend to think women were viewed as property or not well regarded in the Old Testament, but this small, yet important, detail in the text, among other texts within this book seems to tell a different story.

Does this surprise you?

---

[99] Ibid., 386.
[100] Hill, Andrew E. and John A. Walton, editors. *A Survey of the Old Testament, Third Edition*, 174.
[101] Hess, Richard S. *The Old Testament: A Historical, Theological, and Critical Introduction*, 149.
[102] Berlin, Adele and Mark Zvi Brettler, editors. *The Jewish Study Bible*, 352.
[103] Ibid.

As we wrap up the Ten Commandments, there is another detail that is noteworthy to pass along. The order of these commands is not without intention and care. We already alluded to the design of the first four commandments applying to our relationship with God and the last six applying to our relationships with others, but another distinction is important to share. This list begins and ends with "bookends" of sorts, with a focus on the interior aspect of our obedience.[104] These would certainly have outward expressions and actions, but their complete obedience by any one of us would be known only by God Himself, as the only one able to look upon our hearts and know them fully.

REFLECTION

Did any one of these commandments (from any of the days) stand out to you more than another? Why do you think that is? Explain.

How does our obedience to any of the Ten Commandments reflect God's character and presence to others around us? How does our disobedience compromise the reflection of His character (and ours)?

---

[104] Motyer, J.A. *The Message of Exodus: The Days of our Pilgrimage.* (Downers Grove, IL: InterVarsity Press, 2005), 216.

Had you considered the importance of the list order within the tenth commandment, about coveting? What have you found yourself most prone to covet? How can you guard against this?

How might Israel hearing God's voice for themselves affect their willingness to accept the laws? (Or did it?)

DAY FIVE

You Heard, the Lord Heard, Walk in Obedience
(Deuteronomy 5:23-33)

It's our last day in Deuteronomy 5.
Today we will remember the day Israel first heard the laws and
we will see their call to walk in obedience to all they received.

~•~•~

Read Deuteronomy 5:23-33.

Moses reminded Israel, once again, of the day they heard God's voice "out of the darkness" while the mountain was "ablaze with fire." He reminded them of their own words confirming that they had seen God's glory and had heard His voice from the fire, and then how quickly they had allowed their fear to overtake them. Can you hear it as well?

Just as strongly as they were convinced God had spoken and had shown His glory, they were fearful and convinced they were about to die by the fire or by hearing the voice of the Lord any longer than they had. They had pleaded with Moses to go and serve as their mediator, to go near to the Lord and so spare them.

What was the Lord's response to this? In verse 28 He says that the people's request is "good," and then declares His longing for Israel's heart to be inclined to fear Him and to keep His commands (though He knows they won't always). He responded to their fear for their lives with a desire for their fear to be for Him alone.

Of course, this "fear" is not understood to be the same in each case. The fear of the Lord is a fear of respect and regard, with an aspect of allegiance towards the object of that fear. It is born of a trust and desire to please the one who is feared. It is regarded in a positive manner.

The fear of dying or facing some other unfortunate circumstance is simply a fear of harm towards oneself or one's status. It could easily keep a person from drawing near to God or from obeying His commands fully (as we saw in the narrative of the spies in Numbers 13). Moses concludes this chapter with the charge to "be careful to do what the Lord has commanded" and to "walk in obedience…so that you may live and prosper…in the land that you will possess" (v32-33). Obedience to God's commands would bring blessing for Israel.

REFLECTION

"A person can live even if God speaks with them." Have we lost some of this reverence and awe at our hearing God's voice in His Word? Explain.

Have you struggled with the concept of fearing the Lord? How can one have a proper regard and trust for the Lord without being completely afraid? What is the balance?

Verse 33 calls Israel to "walk in obedience" that they may live and prosper. Is there a specific sphere of your life in which you are being called to walk in greater obedience? Explain.

WEEK FOUR NOTES

WEEK FIVE

Remember: A Work of Heart

CHAPTER 6

Last week, we joined Moses on the mountain to hear from the Lord and we considered the goodness of the law from God. This week, we will look at the heart behind that law and find a God who desires the heart of His people in love and obedience–and who seeks to form their hearts over a lifetime and across generations.

We will see how the covenant of God is a "work of heart."

DAY ONE

Reflective Reading
(Deuteronomy 6)

Today we will take time to read the entire chapter we are studying this week.

~•~•~

Read Deuteronomy 6 (in its entirety).

It's always a good study practice to read through a chapter in its entirety, in one sitting, without interruption. This text is an especially digestible size with which to do this.

REFLECTION

Did anything stand out to you in this reading? Any repeated words or themes? Any questions you have?

What was Moses calling the people to do? Is this different from anything we've read so far?

WEEK FIVE – DAY ONE

What did you learn about the character of God from today's reading? Is this different from anything we've read so far?

What do you hope to learn about this chapter this week?

What did you learn that you can share with someone else today?

DAY TWO

Hear the Lord
(Deuteronomy 6:1-3)

Today we will begin to move our way slowly through the text.

~ • ~ • ~

Read Deuteronomy 6:1-3.

"The commands" refer back to the Ten Commandments Moses had just given them, commands they were to observe in the land they were going to possess.

Why does Moses say he had been directed to teach them the laws (v2)?
1) _____
2) _____

These laws brought benefits and promises for present *and* future generations. Through the law, their children's children would fear the Lord.

We touched on what the "fear of the Lord" means in last week's homework. That concept will gain momentum in this week's homework.

For the faithful Israelite to hear the promise that their children and their children after them would fear the Lord and follow His decrees and commands pointed to a legacy of faith. This would be an honor and delight to any Jewish parent. (Indeed, it is the honor and delight of any Christian parent today! The apostle John said in one of his letters, regarding his spiritual children following God, "I have no greater joy than to hear that my children are walking in the truth" (3 John 1:4).

And, to hear that they would enjoy a long life–to be able to enjoy seeing their children and their children's children, walking in God's ways and serving Him would, undoubtedly, be a blessing!

In verse 3, Moses spoke of further blessing…blessing which more specifically pointed to the promises God had made with Israel's ancestors hundreds of years prior.

What would happen for Israel if they obeyed the commands (v3)? _____
_____
_____

They would increase greatly. That was a promise that had been woven throughout the Pentateuch and impressed upon the hearts of the Israelites throughout their upbringing. The God of Israel had promised Abraham that He would make him a great nation and cause him to increase greatly (Gen 12:2; 17:2). He promised Abraham he would have descendants more numerous than the stars in the sky (Gen 15:5). This was a promise with which Israel was well-acquainted. It was an important piece of the covenant God had made with Abraham.

The other major component of the promise God made in His covenant with Abraham was the promise that he (and his offspring) would inherit the land of Canaan (Gen 12:7; 15:7; 17:8). This was the land Israel was now preparing to enter!

And, when God first called Moses, He declared that He was coming down to rescue the Israelites from Egypt, and to bring them into a land "flowing with milk and honey" (Exodus 3:8). Throughout their desert wandering the nation would have heard this phrase (and this promise) about the land the Lord was calling them to.

As Israel heard Moses reference all these things in this one sentence, they would certainly be called to depth of emotion and surety that the Lord who promised all of these things would surely do the same for them if they would "be careful to obey" (v3). Israel knew their God and His Word. They knew His promises and they knew their own failures. And yet, Moses was reminding them that the Lord was keeping His promises to them even now.

REFLECTION

With your understanding of the term so far, how do you, or could you, "fear the Lord" in practice? How do your children (or others around you) see your fear of the Lord and active faith?

Moses just spent an entire chapter emphasizing the importance of Israel's obedience to God's commands. Does this feel repetitive? (Just wait!) Given what we've read so far, why do you think he repeats the need for obedience again here? How is this repetition building upon itself throughout the book thus far?

How does the promise of land and its thread through the Pentateuch bring you hope as you wait on the Lord today? (Or does it?) Israel waited more than 440 years for this promise to come to fruition. How does this offer you perspective as you wait on the Lord?

DAY THREE

Hear, O Israel—The Shema
(Deuteronomy 6:4-9)

Today we will study a section of Scripture that is especially highly regarded by Jewish peoples.

~•~•~

Read Deuteronomy 6:4-9.

This section of Scripture is called *The Shema*. The Shema is so named because of the first word of the text which in Hebrew is *sema (*translated "hear" in English).[105] It called the Jewish believer to "exclusive loyalty to Yahweh," much like a confession of faith.[106] As such, some scholars have likened it to a "John 3:16 of the Old Testament."[107] It is at the heart of Jewish belief.

The Shema was, and is still, recited each morning and evening by devout Jews.[108] It serves as a regular reminder of the covenant call upon and responsibility of each follower of God.

The Shema is a call to "love the Lord your God with all your heart and with all your soul and with all your strength" (v5). It is a call to offer wholehearted loyalty and allegiance to the one true God. Its inclusion in the Deuteronomy document is not only important from a religious standpoint, but it is another way this book mirrors the suzerain/vassal treaties of the ancient Near East and so would have made cultural sense to nearby nations and Israel herself.[109] This, of course, is not as obvious to our Western understanding.

But, far different from the treaties of those around them, this call to covenant allegiance to the Lord also had an emotional component to it. Theologian Bill Arnold says that "God's love for Israel is typically granted as an emotional fundamental of the Bible, and so we should admit

---

[105] Berlin, Adele and Mark Zvi Brettler, *The Jewish Study Bible,* 361.
[106] Ibid.
[107] Holsteen, Nathan D. and Michael J. Svigel. *Exploring Christian Theology,* 143.
[108] Wiersbe, Warren W. *The Bible Exposition Commentary Old Testament: The Pentateuch, Genesis-Deuteronomy,* 388.
[109] Arnold, Bill T. "The Love-Fear Antinomy in Deuteronomy 5-11." *Vestus Testamentum,* 61 no 4, 2011, 554.

as much for Israel's love for God."¹¹⁰ Israel's call to be loyal to God in the call to love Him was not only a call to obedience and duty, but a call to respond to God's great love with love in return.

And, it was from that mutual love, that obedience would flow. (We can see an example of this principle in the words of Jesus when He says, "If you love me, you will obey my commands" John 14:15.)

How do you love the Lord your God with all your heart, soul, and strength? What does that look like?

The Rabbinic tradition interprets this to mean "willing to give one's life for God" (soul).¹¹¹ It also interprets "strength" as wealth and property, so loving with all one's strength could mean being willing to give one's wealth and property for God.¹¹² This is far more than simply a physical strength.

In verse 6, Moses instructed the Israelites to have these commandments on their hearts. The heart was seen as a "center of emotions" but *also* the "center of reason and intellect."¹¹³ As such, the "love of God alone was to guide each person's every action, thought, and movement."¹¹⁴ And, by doing this, they would begin to "mimic Yahweh's intentionality as stewards and image bearers, seeking His glory as a testimony to the nations."¹¹⁵ Indeed, the remainder of this chapter, and the entirety of the book of Deuteronomy, would reiterate this call upon their hearts.

As the passage continues, Moses reminded the Israelites to teach the commands to their children and to surround themselves with reminders of the law (v7-9). This section of text points to the importance of passing along our faith to the next generation. Walter Brueggeman says that "Deuteronomy always has its eyes on the children, on the coming generation," and this section is further evidence of that.¹¹⁶ (We've already seen this in verse 2 and in other chapters within Deuteronomy.) To impress God's commands to their children, to talk about them, and to have them as symbols on their bodies and houses was a command to have the Lord God and His commands "permeate every sphere of the life of man."¹¹⁷

---

[110] Ibid., 558.
[111] Berlin, Adele and Mark Zvi Brettler, *The Jewish Study Bible*, 362.
[112] Ibid.
[113] Craigie, P.C. *The New International Commentary on the Old Testament: The Book of Deuteronomy*. (Grand Rapids, MI: William B. Eerdmans Publishing Company, 1976.), 227.
[114] Ryken, Leland, James C. Wilhoit, and Tremper Longman, III. *Dictionary of Biblical Imagery*, 205.
[115] Smith, Richard L. "Such a Heart as This: The Intellectual Implications of Deuteronomy 5:29," 34.
[116] Brueggeman, Walter. *Abingdon Old Testament Commentaries: Deuteronomy*, 85.
[117] Craigie, P.C. *The New International Commentary on the Old Testament: The Book of Deuteronomy*, 170.

WEEK FIVE – DAY THREE

One especially important piece of this entire section of text is the call reminding Israel, "The Lord our God, the Lord is one" (v4).[118] Why might this have been an important declaration?

As we've already considered, the peoples of the lands surrounding the Israelites served many gods. But the God of Israel was the One true God, and He would share His glory and worship with no other gods. Understanding Yahweh as one not only pointed to Him as the only one worthy of worship, but also as the one supreme in rule and reign.[119]

Imagine the power, strength, and encouragement to one's very soul when they make this declaration each and every day, at the beginning of the day and at the close of the day, "Hear, O Israel: The Lord our God, the Lord is one."

He is the one who rescued and delivered them. He is the one who has kept His promises to them. He is the one who has led them and provided for them. He is the one who has, in His love and grace, given them His law to reveal Himself to them and to teach them. He is the one who will continue to carry them into the new land, giving them victory over their enemies and every good thing He has prepared for them. He is the one who will give them rest, hope, and a future. He is the only one worthy of their worship and praise.

And we can declare the same. Take a moment to read the above paragraph again, replacing every occurrence of "them" and "their" with "me" and "my" as a personal exercise to encourage your heart right now.

---

[118] Another important facet of this "one" in the original Hebrew language is the way it provides the possibility for "plurality within unity." The Hebrew "Elohim" used here means "powerful ones" and is plural in nature, but it is paired with singular verb tenses in this text and elsewhere. This "oneness" may be more of a "unity," which can support our Christian doctrine of the Trinity. God is "one" in essence, though three in person. Holsteen, Nathan D. and Michael J. Svigel. *Exploring Christian Theology*, 144-145.

[119] Craigie, P.C. *The New International Commentary on the Old Testament: The Book of Deuteronomy*, 227.

REFLECTION

Israel is called to tie God's commandments as symbols on their hands and bind them on their foreheads. How is this different from the warning against images or icons in chapter 4 and in the second commandment? How would having these symbols be helpful to the Israelites as they sought to remember the commandments the Lord had given them?

Have you placed symbols/reminders of God's commandments and Word in your home? On your person? What are some ways you've sought to have reminders of God's truth around you? How have these helped? Are there certain verses or "themes" you seem most drawn to, to help your heart remember? Share.

What are some ways to impress God's commandments upon our children? What does this look like in practice on a day-to-day basis? How can we obey this principle even if we do not have children of our own?

Do you see a correlation between verse 4 and the 1st commandment (discussed in chapter 5, last week)? How do these work together to remind Israel of who their God is?

How does our current world struggle with the concept of the Christian God being the one true God? How can we guard and prepare our hearts to more readily and accurately declare and live out the truth that our God is the only one worthy of worship?

CREATIVE EXERCISE: One way the call to write God's commands on the doorframes of their houses has been applied in a literal sense in Jewish homes over the years is through the use of mezuzahs. These are small rectangular boxes that are created with a hollow space in which a small scroll containing the words of the Shema is contained. They are affixed to the door frames (sometimes just to main external doors and sometimes also to the internal doors of bedrooms and other important dwelling spaces) to remind the believer of the call to live for God.

Consider creating a mezuzah for your home. Use materials of your choosing to create a small box to affix to your door frame. Write (or type) out the Shema and roll it to be placed inside the box. Consider holding a special ceremony with gathered friends or family. Set aside time together to read through the text of Deuteronomy 6 and the Shema. Talk to your friends and your family about the importance of this text– about what it meant to Israel then and what it means to us as followers of Christ today. Explain the hope that this symbol will serve as a reminder to each of you within your family/home (and to those who come and go and may ask about its meaning) of your desire to live out your faith in obedience to the Lord and His Word.

(Note: This is simply an exercise; we are not held to any obligation to affix mezuzahs or any other symbols in our homes, but I do believe there is power in some physical engagement with God's Word and certainly in having a visual reminder of the things we have learned along the way.)

DAY FOUR

Do Not Forget
(Deuteronomy 6:10-19)

One thing we can remember: we are prone to forget.
We need to be reminded time and time again,
by others and by ourselves. Today, Moses
will seek to prepare Israel for this particular need.

~•~•~•~

Read Deuteronomy 6:10-19.

In this section, Moses continues to give Israel instruction to be careful to "not forget the Lord" when they enter the land He had sworn to them. He cited the many things they would receive as gifts–fully developed, ready, and matured. They would not have to work to create any of these items, nor would they have to wait for any of them to be productive…vineyards and olive groves would be fruitful, and their every need would be provided. And, therein, lay the danger. Christopher Wright asserts, "fullness can lead to forgetfulness, especially forgetfulness of where they came from and what Yahweh had rescued them from."[120] Israel may very well become so "full" of these good things that she would forget where she came from–specifically the land of slavery from which the Lord had delivered her, and ultimately the Lord Himself who gave them every good thing and was worthy of their thanks and praise.

Moses called Israel to fear God and to serve Him alone (v13). We already considered that to fear God is to offer Him our reverence, worship, and obedience, but theologian Bill Arnold describes this fear as more than basic obedience–he says it is a radical obedience.[121] This would be an obedience that regarded God, and His will, as most important. This flows well from the teaching we considered yesterday about being willing to give up one's life, wealth, and strength for God. Radical obedience would be willing to give up all of these things simply to obey. And, in keeping with that teaching and thinking, it is the love (from God and for God) that makes this type of obedience "a blessing and not a burden."[122]

---

[120] Wright, Christopher J.H. *Understanding the Bible Commentary Series: Deuteronomy*, 101.
[121] Arnold, Bill T. "The Love-Fear Antinomy in Deuteronomy 5-11," 565-566.
[122] Wiersbe, Warren W. *The Bible Exposition Commentary Old Testament: The Pentateuch, Genesis-Deuteronomy*, 394.

WEEK FIVE – DAY FOUR

In verse 16, Moses charged the nation to not put the Lord to the test as they had at Massah. This surely would have evoked emotion in the hearts of the Israelites. They knew what Moses was speaking about; they had lived through the experience and those who had not (or who might not remember personally) had the detailed stories to remind them.

Let's become acquainted with this story as well.

Read Exodus 17:1-7.

What did Israel say as they grumbled against Moses? (v3) _____

_____

In this narrative, during their wandering, Israel became thirsty and began to grumble against Moses, and question his leadership and their God. Moses cried out to God who, in His mercy and discipline, through Moses, provided water for the entire nation from a rock. The place was called "Massah" because the people "tested" their God and also "Meribah" which means "quarreling."

What did the Israelites say when they quarreled? (v7) _____

_____

It's interesting that Moses cited this story just after he warned Israel not to follow other gods and reminded them that the Lord "who is among you" is a jealous God whose anger would burn against them (v15). Lest they question or forget that the Lord is with them, Moses would remind them through their own story of testing.

Israel must never forget their good God who had gone before them and provided for them in the wandering–the good God who would lead them into the good land He had promised. They could remember and rely upon the God who would move against their enemies in the land they were entering. Their remembering of the past would prepare and empower them for the present.

REFLECTION

How could God's generous gifts to Israel make it easy for them to forget that He was the one who delivered them? How can our comfort make us more prone to forget? Is there anything we can do to guard against this?

How had Israel put the Lord to the test at Massah? How can we be prone to put the Lord to the test in our lives today?

How have you followed God in radical obedience? What has that looked like? Or, if you're not sure that you have, what might it look like? How can you be prepared to obey in radical ways in the future?

DAY FIVE

Discipleship: A Legacy of Faith
(Deuteronomy 6:20-25)

Today we will see the promise of a legacy of faith, and a hope for righteousness.

~•~•~

Read Deuteronomy 6:20-25.

This passage revisits the importance of passing along a legacy of faith and wonder to the next generation, that they may know about God's deliverance and understand the motivation behind God's stipulations, decrees, and laws. Israel was to give her eyewitness testimony to the next generation, that they might also fear the great Lord who had delivered them.

How was the Israelite to answer their son's question? (v21) _____

_____

The questioning by the son in verse 20 echoes the Haggadah tradition within the Passover ceremony, where the family is seated at the table to celebrate the Passover feast and the son asks prescribed questions to help the elder family members tell the Exodus story of deliverance. (Passover was an annual remembrance of the night the angel of death had been sent by God to destroy the firstborn male in every household in Egypt except those who had followed God's orders to prepare their doorposts with a covering of blood. Israel had followed God's orders and had been passed over. They were ready to take flight from Egypt and quickly fled when the grieving Pharaoh finally relented and told Moses to "take his people and go.")

Similar to the Passover celebration, and in reference to the Passover event, the Consecration of the Firstborn reveals many parallels to this passage and Israel's call to remember her past to affect her present.

Read Exodus 13:1-16.

How was the Israelite to answer the son's question? (v14) _____
_____

That is quite an echo of the earlier verse.

But do you also hear the echoes of this entire chapter of Deuteronomy contained in this section of text? Israel needed to remember this story of their deliverance. Israel needed to remember this story of their mighty and awesome God. Israel needed to remember that their God had "brought [them] out" ...to "bring [them] in" (6:23). Moses was reminding them of their story–of God's story–and the importance of "reminding" their children of the things they had not seen themselves, so they could receive their parents' story–their parents' testimony of grace–as their own.

Similarly, we have a call to remember the story of our deliverance. We have a call to remember how the Lord brought us out of the land of slavery. And, similarly, we have been entrusted to share this with the next generation, that they might receive Jesus and experience a testimony of grace of their own. Are you ready to share your story?

REFLECTION

How do you take the time to answer questions of faith from a "younger person" (younger chronologically or spiritually)? How can you be prepared to answer these questions?

Why do "younger people" seem more willing to ask questions about the meaning of things? Do we lose our curiosity or our humility or willingness to ask what about what we don't yet understand? Why is that?

Building on the first question in this section…How would a "younger person" benefit from hearing your testimony of God's deliverance and grace in your life? Have you shared your testimony with someone else before? Take a few minutes to make a list of various ways you could point to His active presence and grace in your life. Consider how you might share these with someone.

How do we understand verse 25 in light of the truth that we "cannot earn our righteousness?" How can keeping God's law be our righteousness?

WEEK FIVE NOTES

WEEK SIX

Remember: A Chosen Nation

CHAPTER 7

This week we move from the heart of the law, and the heart of the covenant, to the "hard" of the law and of claiming the promise. This week we will see Israel's call to be set apart from the nations in the land they are entering. We will see mention of destruction of people and places to fulfill God's promises.

We will likely squirm, and we may be tempted to skip over these portions of the text. We can feel ill-suited for war texts, and those that reveal our good God calling for destruction of others can make us especially uncomfortable. We may well need to pause and take a breath and that's okay.

It's my prayer that, when we finish this week's work, we will be able to see glimpses of God's provision and care, and His goodness and grace, even in these difficult words.

DAY ONE

Reflective Reading
(Deuteronomy 7)

Today we will read the entire chapter and answer some reflective questions.

~•~•~

Read Deuteronomy 7 in its entirety.

REFLECTION

Do you see any repeated words or phrases in this text?

Did you encounter anything confusing or disturbing?

Do you have questions about this text? What do you hope to learn about this text this week?

DAY TWO

Driving Out the Nations
(Deuteronomy 7:1-6)

Okay. You've read through the entire chapter one time and
have (hopefully) started processing your initial thoughts and feelings
about this piece of the covenant land promise.
Now, it's time to begin working through the text a little bit at a time.

~•~•~

Read Deuteronomy 7:1-6.

"When the Lord" …Moses turns their hearts and minds toward the time when they will enter the land God has promised, and when they do, the Lord will go before them, driving out "many nations" (seven are listed here). The God of Israel going before them to drive out the foreboding enemies? We can appreciate that declaration, right?

I think it's the next "when" that makes us uncomfortable. It's the "when" that includes an actionable point for Israel that makes us squirm.

> **When the Lord your God has delivered them over to you and you have defeated them, then** _____
> _____. (v2a)
>
> **Make no treaty with them and show them** _____. (v2b)

I suspect this is the picture of the God of the Old Testament some of our hearts have feared over time. The English words "destroy totally" are translated from the Hebrew word *herem*. *Herem* (in total-kill language as we considered in week two in the battles of King Sihon and King Og) is best considered to be understood as a metaphor for "rigorous separation from [in this case] the Canaanite religion."[123] Similar language was often used in ancient Near East war literature, and

---

[123] Moberly, R.W.L. "Theological Interpretation of an OT book: a response to Gordon McConville's Deuteronomy." *Scottish Journal of Theology*, 56 no 4, 2003, 523.

within those instances and within Israel's use it typically communicated: (1) a decisive win, (2) the enemy no longer posing a threat, and/or (3) armed forces having surrendered or fled.[124] Our Western ears want to be plugged and shut up when we consider massive bloodshed, but we must remember, though it was not routine, God had His reasons for giving this command when He did.

Canaan was not innocent. They had "opportunity to recognize and know" Israel's God, but they chose to continue to follow their own gods.[125] The God of Israel would "remove Canaan from the Promised Land because of their sin."[126] He would go before Israel to drive out many nations who refused to follow Him. And it would be the ones who refused to leave that would be destroyed by Israel. It was those stubborn and rebellious people who would be shown no mercy. Philip Stern considers this a "negative counterpart to the first commandment, to serve only Yahweh," and states (as we will see in the next section) that "because God is a jealous God, He will tolerate no rival practice."[127]

What else does God tell them to do? Let's take a look.

List the remaining commands God gives the Israelites (v2, 3, & 5).

What reason(s) does Moses give for these commands (v4 & 6).

Israel was not to make treaties with the nations of Canaan, nor to intermarry with them. Christopher Wright explains that making treaties with them would be for political gain and could "require recognition of the other nation's gods" and intermarrying could be leveraged for political and social gain, which would surely also bring treaties and "introduction to religious practices that would lead to idolatry."[128] These arrangements would be far from simple or innocent for Israel.

Israel was also called to destroy all of the other nations' religious spaces and tools for worship (v5). They were to serve no gods other than Yahweh Himself, thus the elimination of these

---

[124] Webb, William J. and Gordon K. Oeste. *Bloody, Brutal, and Barbaric? Wrestling with Troubling War Texts*, 14.
[125] Wiersbe, Warren W. *The Bible Exposition Commentary Old Testament: The Pentateuch, Genesis-Deuteronomy*, 378.
[126] Webb, William J. and Gordon K. Oeste. *Bloody, Brutal, and Barbaric? Wrestling with Troubling War Texts*, 64.
[127] Brueggeman, Walter. *Abingdon Old Testament Commentaries: Deuteronomy*, 95.
[128] Wright, Christopher J.H. *Understanding the Bible Commentary Series: Deuteronomy*, 110.

methods of idolatry, even after the people had been removed, was of urgent importance. Indeed, "the underlying objective in biblical holy war is *not* the killing of people or the killing of *all* of the enemy" but in "accentuating eschatological hope of someday eliminating idolatry from the land entirely and enjoying the worship of Yahweh exclusively."[129] (Note: eschatological is an academic word for "end times/final judgment.") This is all a fancy way of saying that biblical holy war was seeking to bring the reality on earth closer to the promised restoration of heaven.

The Lord had called Israel to wholehearted devotion (see chapter 6), and their lives were to reflect His holiness. Verse 6 called them "a people holy to the Lord," meaning they "were separated for and belonged to Him."[130] They were God's "treasured possession." They were not to be enticed by the world and its ways, and certainly not by its gods.

Walter Brueggeman calls verse 6 the "thesis statement" of this chapter and of the "theology of Deuteronomy" as a whole.[131] It was because of their being "holy to the Lord" and having been "chosen" and God's "treasured possession" that they were called to be separate. Warren Wiersbe specifically states that "separation meant safety" for Israel at this point in their newness as a nation.[132] They would need to be cautious in their fellowship with the world and its ungodly practices.

Israel had already struggled with rebellion and idolatry in her past, but God had been merciful and had kept His promise to them to enter the land. His going before them, driving out the nations, and helping them to destroy those (larger and stronger) who remained, along with their idolatrous ways, was further evidence of His mercy. They would have the opportunity to live as God's holy people in the land He had given them, solely because they were His treasured possession.

As Christians, we have been called to go into the world and share the good news of Jesus with others. But even in that, we, like the Israelites, have also been called to be mindful of our relationships with others. 2 Corinthians 6:14 charges us to not be "unequally yoked with unbelievers." Much like Israel and her call to not enter into treaties or intermarry with those who followed other gods from the surrounding nations, we are to be cautious about how we may be influenced by those closest to us. We, too, must protect our hearts and minds as we seek to love the Lord our God with our heart, soul, mind, and strength. Matthew Henry specifically says, "We are in danger of having fellowship with works of darkness if we take pleasure in fellowship with those that do those works."[133]

---

[129] Webb, William J. and Gordon K. Oeste. *Bloody, Brutal, and Barbaric? Wrestling with Troubling War Texts*, 14.
[130] Brueggeman, Walter. *Abingdon Old Testament Commentaries: Deuteronomy*, 95.
[131] Ibid.
[132] Wiersbe, Warren W. *The Bible Exposition Commentary Old Testament: The Pentateuch, Genesis-Deuteronomy*, 391.
[133] Henry, Matthew. *A Commentary on the Whole Bible: Volume 1, Genesis to Deuteronomy*, 757.

REFLECTION

Was the idea that these destruction passages point to a merciful God a new concept for you? How does this encourage your understanding of God's goodness and mercy?

Consider your relationships. Do your closest relationships share your desire to follow God? Do you have a good community of people who help you grow in your walk with the Lord? How can you be purposeful in protecting your heart for God? (Note: We don't recommend you "totally destroy" others for righteousness' sake, especially within the covenant of marriage–this was a command for Israel in a specific time and place, for a specific reason– but how can you be intentional within your many relationships in strengthening your wholehearted allegiance and submission to the Lord?)

As we considered verse 6, that Israel was a "people holy to the Lord" and a "treasured possession," did you consider any other places in Scripture you may have heard this concept? Read 1 Peter 2:9-10. What does Peter tell the Christian believers they are? Does this sound familiar? Peter challenged the believers to let their conduct in the world be a witness of their being set apart for the Lord. How was Israel challenged to live this out in the Promised Land? How will you live this out today?

DAY THREE

The Lord's Choosing; By Grace Alone

Deuteronomy 7:7-10)

There was nothing impressive about Israel to cause the Lord to choose them as objects of His affection. He simply loved them and kept His covenant of love and His oath with them over all generations.

Read Deuteronomy 7:7-10.

What a picture of grace, right here in Moses' sermon to the Israelites! The Lord had chosen Israel, not because of any merit or strength of their own, but simply because of His love for them.

Moses will remind them of this truth (particularly in contrast to the wickedness of Canaan) again in chapter 9, but within this portion of text we see his care to be sure they know their great value and worth in the eyes of their God. The same God who was well-acquainted with their failures in the past, chose them simply because of His love for them. *The Expositor's Bible Commentary* says, "It is the character of God rather than any excellencies in the people that accounts for the choice [of Israel]."[134] And the same is true for us.

Interestingly, Yahweh's love for Israel was first introduced here in verse 8; it was not expressed anywhere else in the Pentateuch.[135] But, here Moses was purposeful to remind the nation of Israel of God's love for them. The same nation that had been called to love the Lord their God with all their heart, soul, and strength could know they were deeply loved by their God.

God had been faithful to Israel, revealing His love and mercy. He had also been just, revealing His judgment on those who hated Him and rebelled against Him. The same God who had faithfully loved and cared for Israel is the same God who had faithfully, and without compromise, carried out His justice and judgment on those who would rebel against Him and His ways.

---

[134] Barker, Kenneth L. and John R. Kohlenberger, III, editors. *The Expositor's Bible Commentary, Abridged Edition: Old Testament.* (Grand Rapids, MI: Zondervan, 1994), 249.

[135] Earl, Douglas S. "The Christian Significance of Deuteronomy 7." *Journal of Theological Interpretation*, 3 no 1, Spring 2009, 42.

This is the message of Deuteronomy 7 and the reason for this "holy war" Israel would find herself in. A just and loving God would allow His judgment to fall on the nations who rebelled against Him, and He would make a way for His chosen people whom He loved.

REFLECTION

How does this picture of love and justice point to a holy and merciful God?

How has God chosen you? Was it because of your righteousness or any qualities that would impress Him? Or were you, like Israel, chosen simply because God loved you and sought you as His own?

The Apostle Paul has some things to say about this. Read Ephesians 2:1-9. How does God's love, mercy, and judgment come into play in this passage and in our gift of salvation in Christ Jesus? How does our story parallel Israel's? How does it differ?

How are you feeling about the war text today? Are you seeing any further mercy within this reality for Israel and for her descendants (which includes us) after her?

DAY FOUR

A Blessed Nation, Set Apart
(Deuteronomy 7:11-16)

In today's text, Moses reminds Israel of the blessing
to come in accordance with their obedience to God's laws.
He reminds them of the covenant blessings God had promised
them all along through their ancestors,
and he warns them again of their need to
be separate from the people of Canaan.

Read Deuteronomy 7:11-16.

This text includes a strong warning for Israel against showing pity to the nations the Lord gives to them. Moses wisely prefaces the warning with a reminder to Israel of the nature of their God–the one who has kept His covenant of love with Israel, and the one who had been promising this land and blessing for generations. Indeed, Moses wisely points to God's love, which is "evident in the way He protects and blesses the people He has chosen."[136] Though Israel had failed many times over their existence, their God had kept His covenant of love and sought to bless them in their new land.

What blessings did God offer Israel (v13-15)?

(Note: It is important that we recognize that, much like the war texts we considered earlier, these blessing texts are spoken with hyperbole/exaggeration of blessing. These would not necessarily be literal expectations—no one childless and every person free from every disease—but these would be overall marks of general care.)

---

[136] Hayes, Katherine M. "The Gift of Land: Instructions Included (Deuteronomy 7-8)." *The Bible Today*, 56 no 3, May-June 2018, 161.

These verses contain echoes of the blessings offered, and repeated, within the book of Genesis. Israel would be well aware of these long-anticipated promises from God. Reminding them of the blessings that awaited them would surely encourage Israel and strengthen them for the battle ahead.

One additional encouragement within these blessings lies within the fact these also all point to blessings of fertility and fruitfulness–in mankind, in creatures, and in the fruit of the land. The nations the Lord would be driving out of Canaan looked to their many gods as the source of fertility and fruitfulness, but even these mighty and undeniable blessings upon Israel when she entered the new land would reveal to Israel and to Canaan that it was Israel's God who ultimately gave these blessings.[137] The blessings upon Israel would testify to the God of Israel as the one true God. Israel could be strengthened in that truth and promise.

REFLECTION

What picture would these promises of blessing (in v13-15) give Israel? How would the parallel between Egypt and Israel's enemies help Israel see the danger in becoming friendly with the nations around them?

---

[137] Berlin, Adele and Mark Zvi Brettler, 363.

How might Israel be tempted to "look on [the other nations] with pity?" How could this compromise their walk and prove a snare to them? Do we face a similar challenge in our call from Christ to love our enemies? How do we reconcile this?

How can it be dangerous for us to look at these pronounced blessings without understanding the literary devices of hyperbole/exaggeration behind them? How might it be dangerous for us to seek to apply these blessings as literal promises in our own lives as believers today?

DAY FIVE

A Nation Unafraid & Unadulterated
(Deuteronomy 7:17-26)

Moses has been delivering encouragement with each paragraph of text in this chapter, and in this section his cries of encouragement and hope reach a far greater crescendo.

~•~•~

Read Deuteronomy 7:17-26.

What may the people say to themselves? (v17)? These nations are _____ _____ than we are. How can _____ drive them out?

Moses spoke to the fear in the people's hearts. They had already wandered in the wilderness an additional 40 years because of their fear of the stronger and larger people in the land they were to enter. He knew they may be battling that same fear yet again.

And so he offered a strong encouragement to "not be afraid," and he began reminding them (again?!) about the ways they had seen for themselves (or had heard for themselves from those who had seen) the many mighty ways their God had performed signs and wonders and had brought them out of Egypt. He assured them their Lord would not abandon them now!

The Lord your God will _____ to all the peoples you now fear. (v19b)

He would do the same to these people; He would deliver Israel from the people they now feared. Moses continued the battle cry.

The _____ will drive out those nations before you, little by little. (v22a).

He reminded Israel that they would not be the ones driving out the nations, but it would be the Lord their God Himself. They did not need to fear; the battle did not rely upon them and their strength, but, rather, upon the Lord and upon His presence and activity.

Did you notice the way the Lord would drive out the nations? Moses told them it would be "little by little," that God would not allow them to "eliminate them all at once, or the wild animals [would] multiply around [them]" (v22). In fact, it would take Israel seven years to gain control of the Promised Land.[138] This would allow for better care of the land with the entrance of this large nation and the fleeing and destruction of the others and would surely allow for better care of Israel as she moved forward in the new land.

One important agent of the Lord's battle plans within this section has been the subject of scholarly debate over the years.

What will God send among the nations as He drives them out? (v20)

What did Moses mean by this? Was this a literal hornet, as in a literal insect? Or was this, too, a battle metaphor? There is ample evidence and reason to validate both considerations.

A literal hornet is quite possible because insects were known to be used as agents of war in the ancient Near East.[139] Additionally, the Lord had sent literal locusts in the plagues against Egypt (Exodus 10). He could certainly send a literal hornet (or many hornets) to drive out nations.

Similarly, though, a metaphorical hornet is quite possible as well. Insects were often used as metaphors for armies in biblical passages (flies in Isaiah 7:18-19 and locusts in Joel 1-2).[140] In addition to the metaphor for invading armies, the hornet may also be metaphorical for panic or depression that sets in.[141] Indeed, the original Hebrew allows for the metaphorical use to describe the "dread that gripped the Canaanites" or the "reports about Israel that spread panic among the Canaanites."[142]

---

[138] Wiersbe, Warren W. *The Bible Exposition Commentary Old Testament: The Pentateuch, Genesis-Deuteronomy*, 393.
[139] Walton, John H., general editor. *Zondervan Illustrated Bible Backgrounds Commentary, Vol 1: Genesis, Exodus, Leviticus, Numbers, Deuteronomy*, 463.
[140] Craigie, P.C. *The New International Commentary on the Old Testament: The Book of Deuteronomy*, 230.
[141] Walton, John H., general editor. *Zondervan Illustrated Bible Backgrounds Commentary, Vol 1: Genesis, Exodus, Leviticus, Numbers, Deuteronomy*, 463.
[142] Phetsanghane, Souksamay K. "What is the [hornet] of Exodus 23:28, Deuteronomy 7:20, and Joshua 24:12?" *Wisconsin Lutheran Quarterly*, 113 no 3, Summer 2016, 181, 184.

Regardless of the literal or metaphorical use of the hornet, as all of these things could surely have gone before Israel and helped to drive out the nations, Israel could be sure the Lord their God would be the one fighting their battle and causing their success.

Moses closed this section with another call to rid the land of idolatry. He specifically tells Israel to burn their gods' images and not to covet the silver or gold that covered their idols. They are to be set apart, with no detestable items or practices in their homes. This was no time to gather plunder that may ensnare them and set them apart for destruction.

REFLECTION

Why might receiving the new land "little by little" be good or important? How might this encourage the Israelites then and the church today? How might receiving the land all at once or rapidly prove poor for Israel?

What are your thoughts about the use of the hornet? Does this bewilder or encourage you? Do you think it more likely a literal or metaphorical allusion? How would the use of a hornet, one that can find enemies in hiding, be a comfort to a nation afraid of the ensuing and continuing battle?

Why might Israel be tempted to take the silver or gold from the Canaanites' idols? How would this command to resist that temptation be a call to love the Lord with their heart, soul, and strength (6:4-5)?

WEEK SIX NOTES

WEEK SEVEN

Remember: The Lord Himself Has Given Everything

CHAPTER 8

This week we don't have any overt war texts to read, or at least not war with outside enemies. This week we will consider the war we have within ourselves with forgetfulness and pride. We'll consider the ways, if we are not careful, our comforts may well lead to our compromise.

DAY ONE

Reflective Reading
(Deuteronomy 8)

Today we will do a reflective reading of the entire chapter in one sitting. Once again, this is a brief chapter, well suited for this exercise.

~•~•~

Read Deuteronomy 8.

REFLECTION

Did anything stand out to you in this reading? Any repeated words or themes?

What was Moses calling the people to do? Is this the same or different from the calls we've considered so far?

What did you learn about the character of God from today's reading?

What do you hope to learn about this chapter this week?

What did you learn that you can share with someone else today?

DAY TWO

Remember the Lord's Testing
(Deuteronomy 8:1-5)

Today we will begin to work through the text you read and consider why it is so important that we not forget the Lord!

~•~•~

Read Deuteronomy 8:1-5.

Overall, this entire chapter, and certainly this section, is a call to remember. (One could easily assert that the entire book of Deuteronomy has been a call to remember!)

Moses gave Israel another history lesson. He called them to remember how the Lord had led them all the way in the wilderness. He called them to remember how the Lord had tested and instructed them and how He had cared for them. He knew that by calling them to "remember another time" he would help them "learn something important about 'this time.'"[143]

> **Why had the Lord tested Israel? (v2) In order to _____**
> **what was in their _____, whether or not they**
> **would _____ .**

Had they passed the test? What had He found in their hearts? How had they kept His commands?

Israel did not pass the test; a generation died in the wilderness because they had failed the test.[144] But a new generation was able to learn from the previous generation's failure and to choose differently as they entered the new land.

> **How did the Lord humble Israel? (v3) He caused them _____**
> **and then _____ them with _____ .**

---
[143] Brueggeman, Walter. *Abingdon Old Testament Commentaries: Deuteronomy*, 105.
[144] Longman, Tremper III. *The Story of God Bible Commentary: Genesis*. (Grand Rapids, MI: Zondervan, 2016), 293.

Why did He humble them and feed them with manna? To teach them that _____ does not live on _____ alone, but on _____!

How had they learned this in their wilderness wandering?

Throughout their wandering, they learned that God provided for them. Through the manna, they learned that "Yahweh is reliable and generous" and they learned "they would be cared for and safe in every circumstance."[145] And through God's commandments and law, they learned "to listen to God's voice and obey in order to thrive and flourish."[146]

In verse 5, after recalling the testing and humbling Israel had endured in the wilderness, Moses asked Israel to "know then in your heart" that as a man disciplines his son, so the Lord your God disciplines you.

What is the difference between discipline and punishment?

Look up the words "discipline" and "punishment" in the dictionary. Write the definitions here.

How was the Lord's treatment of Israel in the years of wandering (and in the test of manna) discipline rather than punishment?

Do you hear how this verse bears an echo to the verse in 1:31 that refers to the Lord as having carried Israel as a father carries a son? Certainly, Israel would hear this tender familial metaphor.

---
[145] Brueggeman, Walter. *Abingdon Old Testament Commentaries: Deuteronomy,* 106.
[146] Smith, Richard L. "Such a Heart as This: The Intellectual Implications of Deuteronomy 5:29," 30.

REFLECTION

Israel was repeatedly called to "remember." How do you help yourself remember important things? What are some methods you use?

Why would Israel need to experience God's discipline before entering the Promised Land?

During their wandering, the Israelites' clothes did not wear out nor their feet swell (v4). Have you considered this great miracle before? Why would this have been important?

DAY THREE

A Picture of the Good Land
(Deuteronomy 8:6-9)

Today we will get a picture of the good land Israel is preparing to enter. Israel will surely grow more excited at the prospect of all the Lord is bringing them to.

~•~•~

Read Deuteronomy 8:6-9.

Moses reminds Israel of the makeup of the land they are preparing to enter.

How does Moses describe the land? A land:

With _____, _____, and _____ _____ gushing out into the valleys and hills (v7)

With _____ and _____, _____ and _____, _____, _____, _____ and _____ (v8)

Where _____ will not be _____ and you will _____ (!)

Where the rocks are _____ and you can dig _____ out of the hills. (v9)

The wilderness in which the Israelites had been wandering did not have an abundance of water. Water would have been "a commodity."[147] As Moses listed the various water sources the

---
[147] Wiersbe, Warren W. *The Bible Exposition Commentary Old Testament: The Pentateuch, Genesis-Deuteronomy*, 396

new land held, and the way they would be "gushing out into the valleys and hills," there is no doubt the Israelites would have been excited by the prospect!

And then, as Moses listed the various foods and abundance of bread that would be available to them, after having lived on manna (and the short-lived quail, see Exodus 16 & Numbers 11) for the last 40 years, the Israelites undoubtedly would have been eager to go in and enter the land.

And, to hear that the land would also have iron and copper, so Israel could build all they needed. What more could they need? They would certainly experience the provision of the land!

REFLECTION

Why would Moses take the time to describe the land to Israel here?

How would this picture of the good land encourage Israel and embolden them to go in and take the land?

How do you stay motivated for long-term goals that seem far off? What role do mental pictures play in your motivation?

How does Scripture help us as Christians have a good picture of the "good land" we will enter into when Jesus returns? One such picture can be seen in Revelation 21:1-9, 22-27. How does this vision of the new heaven encourage you in obedience and faith as you follow Jesus today?

DAY FOUR

God's Goodness & Grace; Warning Against Pride
(Deuteronomy 8:10-18)

Today we will heed Moses' warning to guard
against pride in the midst of prosperity.

~•~•~

Read Deuteronomy 8:10-18.

Moses warned Israel against forgetting the Lord and failing to observe His commands. He suggested they should praise the Lord when they have eaten and are satisfied (v10). Does this create a familiar image for you?

It is common within Christian tradition to offer a prayer of thanksgiving and grace *before* eating a meal. Interestingly, in the Jewish tradition it is common to offer a prayer of thanksgiving and grace *after* eating a meal (perhaps in keeping with this very verse).[148] In both instances, the prayer of thanksgiving is offered as an act of gratitude to God and an acknowledgement of Him as the giver of every good gift, but there is an interesting perspective within the Jewish tradition of stopping to remember and thank God for the fullness of our bellies when we have been satisfied.

When would Israel need to be careful not to forget the Lord? (v12-13)
- When you eat and are _____
- When you build _____ _____ and settle down
- When your herds and flocks _____ _____ (gain assets)
- When your silver and gold _____ and _____ you have is _____

---
[148] Scherman, Rabbi Nosson and Rabbi Meir Zlotovitz. *The Stone Edition: The Chumash*, 984.

What would happen if they failed to praise the Lord along the way and remember Him? (v14)
- Then, your heart will become _____ and you will _____ the Lord your God who _____ you out of _____, out of the land of _____.

"Success in Canaan would tempt [Israel] to forget the wilderness lesson of complete dependence upon God," and success can tempt any one of us to forget the lessons of dependence we have learned as well.[149]

Have you experienced this in your own life? How? _____
_____
_____
_____
_____
_____
_____

How was the wilderness described? (v15-16)
- Vast and _____
- Thirsty and _____
- With venomous _____ and _____
- Water from a _____
- _____ to eat

This was a very different image from that of the coming Promised Land.

Moses warned Israel they would be prone to forget the Lord as they experienced the prosperity and abundance of the good land. They could easily become prideful and think they had somehow brought all of this goodness onto themselves. They could easily forget that the "earth is the Lord's and everything in it" (Psalm 24:1).

---

[149] Berlin, Adele and Mark Zvi Brettler, *The Jewish Study Bible*, 363.

REFLECTION

How does the wilderness contrast with the "good land" we studied on day 3? How does this contrast with the list of the reality they would experience in verses 12 and 13?

How does forgetfulness lead to pride? How is forgetfulness rooted in pride?

How would pausing to give thanks for your food *after* you have eaten and are satisfied affect your heart of gratitude?

"Counting our blessings" is an important discipline in guarding our heart against forgetfulness and pride. Have you kept a gratitude journal? Consider keeping a gratitude journal for the remaining weeks of this study, listing five things each day you are thankful for–things you have received, ways you've seen God's goodness or presence in your day, reflections of His grace. Share some of your entries with your small group each week.

DAY FIVE

Warning: Judgment Awaits Forgetful & Idolatrous
(Deuteronomy 8:19-20)

Moses has been warning Israel against forgetting their God throughout this chapter but, in these verses, he specifically calls out the judgment and destruction that will be theirs if they, indeed, forget their Lord and walk in pride and ignorance of the goodness of their God.

Read Deuteronomy 8:19-20.

Judgment would come upon Israel just as it had for the nations God judged before them as they entered the good land. Israel could not expect to always be spared if they forgot the Lord and followed other gods. They would need to guard against forgetting their Lord and following other gods in the new land.

There was a very real danger in forgetting the Lord once they entered the new land, as they would no longer "see God's presence and daily miracles" as they had in the wilderness.[150] Without the daily provision of manna or the regular visual of the cloud and the fire, it would be easy for Israel to forget God's still constant presence and provision.

In yesterday's lesson, we spoke about the importance of cultivating gratitude in one's heart to guard against forgetfulness. This is also important in guarding against idolatry, as "idolatry begins in the heart when gratitude to the Giver is replaced by greediness for the gifts."[151] Israel could see this in their day, and I believe we can see this in ours.

---

[150] Scherman, Rabbi Nosson and Rabbi Meir Zlotovitz. *The Stone Edition: The Chumash*, 938.
[151] Wiersbe, Warren W. *The Bible Exposition Commentary Old Testament: The Pentateuch, Genesis-Deuteronomy*, 397.

REFLECTION

How would God judge the nations before Israel in the Promised Land? Should this prove a deterrent to Israel's forgetting the Lord?

How do these warnings apply to us today? How can we be tempted to follow other gods?

How do grace and mercy come into play in passages and warnings such as this? How do these warnings help us better see the grace and mercy of God in His relationship with us

WEEK SEVEN NOTES

WEEK EIGHT

Remember: Not Righteous, But Rebellious, and Yet Redeemed

CHAPTER 9

If chapter 8 was a warning against pride, chapter 9 is a step in the safeguarding of that aim. Moses will remind Israel they were not chosen because of their own righteousness or goodness and will offer evidence to support that all they are preparing to do has been a gift of grace. One scholar declares, "the overall theme of Deuteronomy is the call for Israel to be a covenant people and to be aware of itself as that," and this chapter within the greater work is an answer to that call.[152]

---

[152] Kroeger, Catherine Clark and Mary J. Evans. *The IVP Women's Bible Commentary*, 88.

DAY ONE

Not Because of Righteousness
(Deuteronomy 9:1-6)

Though the Lord would give victory over her enemies,
Israel was not chosen to inherit the land
because of her righteousness.

~•~•~

Read Deuteronomy 9:1-6.

As Moses has done throughout his sermon, he took a moment to remind Israel that the Lord is the one who will go ahead of them and battle with the "greater and stronger" nations in the land He is giving them. They cannot seem to hear this often enough; they can be prone to fear (these people are giants, and there are a lot of them!) and benefit greatly from the assurance that the Lord will be with them and will subdue their enemies on Israel's behalf.

And, in a subtle but important way, he prepared Israel for what is coming next in his speech when he provided the picture of God going before them "like a devouring fire" (v3). This is not a literal fire (though it could include that), but a reference to God's active work to cleanse the land of idolatry and evil. Just two chapters ago, in chapter 7, Moses had instructed the Israelites to burn the enemies' idols and images in the fire to purge the land of unholy worship. He had reminded Israel that participation in idolatry would cause God's anger to burn against them. All Moses was about to share with Israel pointed to that same consuming-fire nature of their God and how it had blessed and disciplined Israel along the way, and how it would be foundational to their victory and obedience in the land to come.

It is not because of your _____ or your _____ that you are going to take possession of their land, but on account of the _____ of these nations…(v5)

On account of the wickedness of these nations. Not because of Israel's righteousness. It is important to remember that "it is not Israel's righteousness but the Canaanites' wickedness that is causing the dispossession in the land."[153] But, perhaps it is even more important to remember that it is actually "because of Canaan's corruption *and* because of God's enduring commitment to His promises to Israel's ancestors."[154] This was not simply a blessing based upon the "lesser of two evils." It was a gift of grace.

It is similar for us. "Salvation for the Israelite, as well as for the Christian, is provided by God alone and not based on man's righteousness."[155] And this important reminder for Israel is an important reminder for us.

The people of Canaan were utterly wicked and profane, serving gods in ways that devalued the lives of others (human sacrifice, temple prostitution, and other sexual immorality in the guise of worship), and refusing to set these false gods and evil practices aside to follow the one true God of Israel. As we considered in chapter 7, these were not people to be pitied or shown mercy. They were met with God's judgment in justice and truth, and Israel would simply be an agent in that judgment. The holy God of Israel would act against injustice and sin.

But, within that truth, Israel must never forget that they are a "stiff-necked people," stubborn in their ways and having proved stubborn towards the Lord as well. (Moses will remind them of that truth in the next section.) And, lest they think themselves deserving favor because of their "righteousness" or merit, they can certainly know that "stubbornness is often incompatible with righteousness."[156] It is difficult, if not impossible, to determinedly seek one's own way and be found following God's way.

---

[153] Barker, Kenneth L. and John R. Kohlenberger, III, editors. *The Expositor's Bible Commentary, Abridged Edition: Old Testament*, 249.
[154] Berlin, Adele and Mark Zvi Brettler, *The Jewish Study Bible*, 363.
[155] Schultz, Samuel J. *Deuteronomy: The Gospel of Love*, 43.
[156] Scherman, Rabbi Nosson and Rabbi Meir Zlotowitz. *The Stone Edition: The Chumash*, 987.

REFLECTION

Israel is described as "a stiff-necked (stubborn) people" in verse 6. This is another way to say they are stubborn. Are there ways you have been stiff-necked or stubborn toward God? What areas prove more difficult for you to surrender your own way? Consider and explain.

There has been a theme of "fire" in relationship to the Lord throughout Deuteronomy. How should the fire be regarded? Is it an image to be feared? An image to be revered? An image to be celebrated as cleansing? What is your response to the image of "fire" thus far?

In chapter 8 and now again in chapter 9, Israel is warned they may "say to [themselves]" statements that assume their own righteousness, strength, or ability has brought their blessing. How does God (through Moses) respond to these presumptuous statements? How can we guard against these types of presumptions in our own lives?

DAY TWO

Rebellion: The Golden Calf
(Deuteronomy 9:7-17)

Lest Israel were to forget their stiff-necked ways,
Moses will remind them of their own wickedness
that roused the anger of the Lord to burn against them.

~•~•~

Read Deuteronomy 9:7-17.

How quickly Israel had turned their hearts from the Lord! While Moses was away, meeting with God and receiving His Word–His law for the nation, which the people had heard with their own ears–the nation of Israel was quick to forget the very God who had brought them to that place.

Let's see the original narrative for more details.

Read Exodus 32:1-10.

How do these additional details reveal their stubbornness all the more?

What does verse 8 tell us about this piece of Israel's story?

"They have been quick to _____ _____
from what I commanded them and have made themselves an _____
cast in the shape of a _____. They have _____
_____ to it and _____
to it and have said, "These are your _____, Israel,
who _____ you up out of Egypt." (Exodus 32:8)

What a contrast here! While Moses, the one who had helped lead them up out of Egypt and had constantly pointed to God as the source of the deliverance, was on Mount Horeb (Sinai) receiving God's law–the commandments that included a commandment against worshiping other gods or forming any type of image of God or any other god, Israel grew forgetful and busied herself fashioning an image to worship and credit for their blessing! (We'll discuss Aaron's involvement in this in tomorrow's lesson, but it is an important detail in this story as well.)

In their impatience and unbelief, they allowed themselves to crave an image like those they had seen in Egypt and acted to ensure they had something before them to worship while they waited for Moses to return.[157]

Returning to the original text in Deuteronomy 9, Moses reminded the people that the Lord's anger had burned against them. He was ready to destroy them (much like the Canaanites) and "blot their name from under heaven," and to make Moses into a nation stronger and more numerous than they" (v14).

This was certainly not a "righteous" nation. They were stubborn, stiff-necked, and sinful. They forgot the way of the Lord and "the way that the Lord had commanded [them]" (v16). Indeed, they were "as deserving of God's destructiveness as the worst of nations," and it was only by God's grace they were spared.[158]

They must never forget this. They must never forget their own sin that demanded judgment.

---

[157] Worship of images of bulls was a common practice to celebrate military prowess and victory in Egypt and other ancient Near Eastern cultures. *NIV Cultural Backgrounds Bible*, 168

[158] Wright, Christopher J.H. *Understanding the Bible Commentary Series: Deuteronomy*, 134.

REFLECTION

Have you ever craved or designed a "golden calf" of your own? Have you hungered for a more visible god or a "reminder" that you are not alone? How can this be dangerous?

In earlier chapters, we considered symbols as visual reminders of God's grace and God's Word (chapter 6), and we recognized the call to ensure we do not create images for worship (chapter 4). How can we know when something is serving as a symbol (and, so, helpful) or when something is serving as an image/idol (and, so, dangerous? (Note: One clarification that may help in your answer is the fact that "symbols, but not images of God, were, and are still, acceptable in Judaism."[159])

---

[159] Middlemas, Jill Anne. "Aniconism and Deuteronomy 4-5," 151.

Does it bother you that God was so quick to say He would destroy Israel and blot out their name from under heaven? How is this a "just" reaction from a "just" God?

DAY THREE

Moses' Intercession
(Deuteronomy 9:18-21)

Israel, in her stubbornness, sinned and revealed herself
not righteous but, instead, worthy of judgment.
But they were not without a mediator to cry out on their behalf.
Today we will see Moses serve as Israel's mediator,
seeking grace and forgiveness, and restoration and life,
for the nation he loves.

~•~•~

Read Deuteronomy 9:18-21.

Moses implored with the Lord on Israel's behalf. He begged the Lord to reconsider, and the Lord listened to him (v19). He would then go before the Lord for 40 days and 40 nights a second time (Exodus 34:28). (It's important to realize that this section has an interweaving of the two realities. This text does not indicate that Moses interceded with fasting and prayer for the Lord to remove His judgment against Israel.[160])

Let's read the intercessory prayer of Moses in its original context.

Read Exodus 32:11-14.

This was while Moses was on Mount Horeb the first time, before he came down to see the golden calf worship and revelry for himself. His response to the Lord's anger and vow of destruction was to cry out on Israel's behalf. He reminded the Lord of His promise to them and of the impact on His Name and His witness to the world if He was seen to have delivered them, only to destroy them before taking them to the Promised Land. The Lord listened to Moses and relented in His judgment against them.

---

[160] Oberst, Bruce. *Bible Study Textbook Series: Deuteronomy*, 147.

In the Deuteronomy text, Moses alluded to God's anger against Aaron and shared that he had interceded specifically for Aaron as well (v20). Aaron was the priest of Israel, and so a leader of their nation, and he had participated fully in the folly of their ways.

In the original text we read yesterday (in Exodus), we do not see evidence of Aaron questioning Israel's desire to make gods for themselves. He did not refuse their request to make them gods, and, in fact, met their requests with a request of his own–that they bring their earrings to him, so he may fashion them a god!

This was their spiritual leader, leading them into idolatry and destruction! (And this same spiritual leader would later deny culpability when Moses confronted him about his part in this sin. (Exodus 32:24) The Lord held him responsible for his actions. Moses did as well, but also implored for God's grace for him. The Lord listened to Moses and spared Aaron's life.

This picture of leadership, even in its errors, is an important reminder to "never underestimate the importance of spiritual leadership that encourages obedience to the Word of God."[161] We need leaders who will stand up for the truth of God's Word. We need leaders who will especially stand up for its truth when we are prone to make it bend to meet our needs or the desires of our hearts. We need leaders who will stand up to us when we begin to step away from God's ways and forget His commands. Aaron failed this test at the foot of Mount Horeb, but his failure can remind each of us as we are called to lead and certainly as we are called to be discerning about the leaders we follow.

Similarly, Moses' great example in spiritual leadership that is willing to go before the Lord in intercession–in grief and repentance–on behalf of the people he has been called to serve and lead, is a valuable reminder for us as well. We are blessed to have leaders who, in humility and love, will go before the Lord to beg for His mercy and grace for us as God's people.

Oh, that we would be leaders worthy of the call, and that we would be blessed to be led by leaders like this!

---

[161] Wiersbe, Warren W. *The Bible Exposition Commentary Old Testament: The Pentateuch, Genesis-Deuteronomy*, 398.

REFLECTION

Why was Moses willing to pray for Israel even in their rebellion?

Have you ever had a leader, authority figure, or even a friend, intercede on your behalf–showing you mercy and grace, caring for your very soul, even when you rebelled or acted foolishly? How did you respond?

Today we considered spiritual leadership and what good leadership and poor leadership looks like. You may have quickly dismissed yourself as a leader, but I encourage you to recognize that each one of us has been called to lead others in spiritual matters. The way you conduct your life–the way you live out the Word of God and obey His commands–is a witness to the Lord's leading in your life, and it affects, and so leads, others in the way of God. So, even informally, you are a spiritual leader of sorts. Knowing this, are there areas you need to grow in, that you might better reflect the leadership ideals we discussed today? Do you need to grow in your boldness to confront disobedience and defend the truth of God's Word? Or do you need to grow in your willingness to intercede for others?

Did today's discussion about leadership bring anyone to mind that has served as a Moses type of leader in your life? One who was willing to stand up for truth (even if needing to confront you in love about your walk) *and* **eager to intercede for those they were called to lead? How have they influenced you? How might you follow their example? Take a moment to intercede for them right now– thank God for their life, for their example, and for your learning from them.**

DAY FOUR

Rebellion: Taberah, Massah, Kilbroth Hattaavah
(Deuteronomy 9:22)

Don't let today's reading fool you. This will not be a "quick" day. This one verse holds much unpacking as we consider three of the places Israel rebelled against God in their wilderness wandering. I promise you that we will be blessed for having slowed our pace to look at these names and places and what they represent in Israel's life with God.

Read Deuteronomy 9:22.

"You also made the Lord angry at Taberah, at Massah, and at Kibroth Hattaavah." These places are listed quickly, and, if we aren't careful, it would be easy to skip over these places that don't hold the same history and recognition for us that they would for Israel.

All three of these places were noteworthy as places of "provocation" of the Lord's wrath against Israel.

Let's look at each of them in greater detail.

1) **Taberah**–this Hebrew word means "burn"

    We can find the story of Taberah in **Numbers 11:1-3.** (I encourage you to read that text now.)

    At Taberah, Israel complained about what they perceived as the "faithlessness" of God. They complained, and the Lord's anger burned. And, so, the Lord burned parts of the camp in response.

    In Taberah, we are reminded that it is a sin to complain.[162]

---
[162] Wiersbe, Warren W. *The Bible Exposition Commentary Old Testament: The Pentateuch, Genesis-Deuteronomy*, 399.

2) **Massah** –this Hebrew word means "testing"

   We find the original stories of Massah in **Exodus 17:1-7** and **Numbers 20:1-13** (note we've already looked at both of these stories in detail in earlier weeks; if you'd like to revisit them, you may; I especially suggest revisiting the Exodus 17 account).

   God's people were thirsty and without water. They did not trust the Lord and complained to Moses and the Lord, asking them both to bring water. Ultimately, Israel did not trust the Lord was among them and at work to meet their needs.

   In Massah, we are reminded to trust the Lord to meet our needs.

3) **Kibroth Hattaavah**–this Hebrew word means "graves of craving/lust"

   We find the original story highlights of Kibroth Hattaavah in **Numbers 11:4-6, 18-20, 31-35.** (I encourage you to read these texts now.)

   At Kibroth Hattaavah, Israel complained about the gift of manna and cried out for meat. God's anger was provoked, and He responded to their complaint by giving them meat for an entire month–until it "came out of their nostrils and they loathed it" (v20). They received what they asked for and in such great measure they no longer desired it. In fact, even as they ate, God sent a plague upon the camp and those who had complained died and were buried (hence the graves).

   In Kibroth Hattaavah, we are reminded not to complain about the gifts of God.

All three of these spaces found Israel crying out to the Lord, but not in reliance and trust; no, they cried out to the Lord in complaint and grumbling. They did not trust the way of the Lord over their own way, and they tested His authority. They provoked God's anger and demonstrated they were neither righteous nor grateful for His faithful provision and care.

REFLECTION

Have you previously recognized grumbling/complaining as a sin against God? How can we walk into this particular sin rather easily? How can we guard and protect against this?

Have you longed for something and then received it, only to eventually realize you no longer appreciated or wanted it (maybe even to eventually despise it)? How did you respond to this reality? Has that experience influenced the way you consider the desires of your heart since? Share.

WEEK EIGHT – DAY FOUR

The experiences we considered today each reveal a provocation of the Lord's anger against Israel in various stages of Israel's wilderness wandering. Israel didn't simply anger the Lord once, learn from it, and never again upset Him. No, Israel's walk was much like ours, in continued growth, failure, repentance, and walking anew again. How can we be encouraged by these reminders (particularly with the added benefit we have in the hope and help of Jesus Christ)? Reflect and share.

DAY FIVE

Rebellion: Kadesh Barnea & God's Grace
(Deuteronomy 9:23-29)

In today's lesson, we will consider a fourth place of Israel's
provocation of the Lord's anger (the provocation that
led to their wandering these many years) and
consider further the incredible role of Moses'
intercession on Israel's behalf.

We must never take the grace of God for granted.
We have each provoked the Lord and deserved
His wrath and judgment, and yet He is able
(and desires) to show us mercy and grace, and to
mold us and make us into a people after His own heart.

Read Deuteronomy 9:23-29.

Let's briefly consider (again) why the anger of the Lord was provoked at Kadesh Barnea. Do you remember what we learned about this place in our study of chapter 1? This was where Israel was camped when they were first told to go in and take the new land. This is the place from which Israel sent the spies into the land, and the place in which Israel heard their report and trembled in fear. This is the place where Israel rebelled against the Lord and refused to trust His Word that said He would go before them, give these nations over to them, and give them rest and prosperity in the Promised Land.

This is why Moses declares, "you have been rebellious against the Lord ever since I have known you" (v24). Indeed, they had revealed much rebellion towards the Lord in their lifetime.

Moses returned to remind Israel about his intercession on their behalf, not likely to point to his activity on their behalf, but more so to point to the grace of God that was given in response to those prayers.

In keeping with Moses' opening statement in this chapter (that Israel was not being given the land because of their own righteousness), Moses was eager to remind Israel that their blessing was only in response to the Lord's covenant promise to their ancestors. It was only possible because the Lord was willing to "overlook the stubbornness of this people, their wickedness, and their sin" (v27b).

Israel was the Lord's inheritance, and it was only because of that truth that He would bring them into theirs.

REFLECTION

In week one, we considered whether we had been fearful in anything the Lord had called us to. It's been seven weeks since we considered that question. How would you answer that question today? Have you previously or recently allowed fear to stop you from doing what you know the Lord has called you to? OR, since we considered that earlier, have you found yourself walking forward in faith over fear to do what you know the Lord has called you to?

How might all of this have been different if Israel had trusted the Lord at Kadesh Barnea, and had gone into the Promised Land when He first commanded them to go? What might those early years in Canaan have been like? What lessons from the wilderness might have been missed?

Have you experienced a delayed answer to a promise (or something you believed to be a "promise") from God? How did you walk through the waiting for the fulfillment of that promise? What valuable lessons did you learn as you waited? How did the waiting affect your joy in the fulfillment? (Or if you are still waiting, how has your heart been encouraged to continue to trust as you wait for that fulfillment?)

WEEK EIGHT NOTES

WEEK NINE

Remember: God's Law Preserved, God's Care Extended

CHAPTER 10

Last week, we recognized God's grace to Israel because of His covenant with them. This week, we will consider how that covenant love and grace given to Israel is to extend to others on God's behalf.

Love of God and love of neighbor is not a New Testament concept alone; rather, it is rooted in the covenant of God and played an important role in Israel's formation as God's people in the new land.

DAY ONE

Reflective Reading
(Deuteronomy 10)

Today we will participate in a reflective reading of chapter 10 in its entirety.

~•~•~

Read Deuteronomy 10.

REFLECTION

Did anything stand out to you in this reading? Any repeated words or themes? Any questions you have?

What was Moses calling the people to do? Is this different from anything we've read so far?

What did you learn about the character of God from today's reading? Is this different from anything we've read so far?

What do you hope to learn about this chapter this week?

What have you learned that you can share with someone else today?

DAY TWO

Second Set of Tablets, Law Preserved
(Deuteronomy 10:1-10)

Moses will walk us through the receipt of the second set of tablets once again today and introduce us to some new details that point to the consistency of God's Word and ways over time.

~•~•~

Read Deuteronomy 10:1-10.

In this account, Moses was told to make an ark to house the stone tablets that contained God's commandments. If you are familiar with the book of Exodus, and the accounts of creating the Tabernacle furnishings, this account in Deuteronomy may initially perplex you.

Read Exodus 37:1-9.

Who is said to have built the ark of the covenant? (v1) _____

How can this be, if Moses has said he was commanded to make the ark and, in Deuteronomy 10:3, says "I made the ark…?" We need not become alarmed by what seems at first blush to be a discrepancy between the texts. In fact, biblical scholar Kenneth Barker asserts, "it is not uncommon that a leader of a venture is said to do something when physical accomplishment is done by someone else."[163] Bezalel would have created the ark under Moses' leadership and direction, and credit for the ark could have been given to either interchangeably. This is another example of the importance of understanding the context within which a text was given, in history, in culture, and in literary structure.

In keeping with the importance of contextual understanding, there is one piece of information about the two stone tablets that you may find fascinating. You may have been picturing these

---

[163] Barker, Kenneth L. and John R. Kohlenberger, III, editors. *The Expositor's Bible Commentary, Abridged Edition: Old Testament*, 251.

tablets to have contained five of the ten commandments on one stone and the other five on the second (perhaps thanks to Hollywood or other images we've seen over the years). But, in fact, the presence of two stone tablets, within historical context, would more likely have pointed to the nature of the covenant treaty which would have had two copies–one for the suzerain/authority and one for the vassal.[164] It would have called for two stones to have identical content so each party would have the conditions of the treaty in their possession. This is thought to be the more likely reason for the two stones Moses would create and eventually house in the ark.

Another important piece of Israel's history is found in the next parenthetical section of the Deuteronomy 10 text.

First, Moses references the transfer of the priesthood from Aaron to his son, Eleazar. (This narrative is shared in Numbers 20:25-28, if you'd like to read the account for yourself).

Second, Moses references the tribe of Levi having been set apart to minister to the Lord.

> **What was the tribe of Levi set apart to do? (v8)**
> - _____ the ark of the covenant to the Lord
> - _____ before the Lord to _____
>   and to pronounce _____ in his name

The tribe of Levi had a set-apart status within the set-apart nation of Israel. We learned in week three that the cities of refuge were found within cities the Levites ministered within. They were present before the Lord in His sanctuary and within the towns where people sought refuge and sanctuary.

And, as the Lord commanded Moses to lead the people into the land He had promised them, He would command the people to minister to others in His name. But first, He would have the Levites lead the people, carrying the ark of the covenant, into the land He had sworn to their ancestors (Joshua 3:3). Israel would not likely miss this picture of God preparing for their entry by preparing the Levites to carry His presence before them.

---

[164] Walton, John H. *The IVP Bible Background Commentary: Genesis-Deuteronomy*, 226.

REFLECTION

Why does God tell Moses to make new stones? Why would they need them? How would their presence in the ark be important to Israel?

Why would God design it to take another 40 days and 40 nights? What might this second period of waiting do for and in Israel?

Why was the tribe of Levi set apart? Read Numbers 18:1-7. Why would Moses focus on their calling and role, particularly just prior to entering the land?

What would the image of the ark of the covenant going into the land before Israel represent to them?

DAY THREE

What Does the Lord Ask of You?
(Deuteronomy 10:12-13)

Today, Moses asks Israel the rhetorical question,
"What does the Lord ask of you?"
He also offers them (and us) the answer.

~•~•~

Read Deuteronomy 10:12-13.

Does this passage sound familiar? It sounds like a recitation of sorts of the Shema in 6:5 (to love God with all one's heart and soul) and the many places Moses has pleaded with Israel to "walk in obedience" to the Lord. It also has a parallel with a verse in Micah 6:8, where the prophet Micah asks and answers the same rhetorical question by stating that Israel is "to act justly and to love mercy and to walk humbly with [their] God."

What five things was Israel called to do? (v12-13)
1)
2)
3)
4)
5)

Does the Lord ask the same of us today? _____

Christopher Wright considers this (and the verses that follow through verse 22) to be "one of the richest texts in the Hebrew Bible."[165] Walter Brueggeman agrees, stating these verses contain the "loveliest, most powerful summations of covenantal theology in the book of Deuteronomy."[166] This simply stated answer to the question sets the trajectory for the heart response of Israel.

Let's pause for greater reflection on this.

---
[165] Wright, Christopher J.H. *Understanding the Bible Commentary Series: Deuteronomy*, 144.
[166] Brueggeman, Walter. *Abingdon Old Testament Commentaries: Deuteronomy*, 128.

REFLECTION

We considered what the Lord asked Israel to do. How are we called to do the same? What does that look like?

Is there any particular one of these commands that is more naturally easy (or difficult) for you to do? Why do you think that is?

How do these all work together, or do they?

What would the church look like if each person sought to answer this call of the Lord in diligent obedience?

DAY FOUR

The Lord: Owner of All, Worthy of Worship
(Deuteronomy 10:14-16)

Today we will walk into the next section of Moses'
answer to the question of what the Lord has called Israel to
and the "how" they will be able to better walk out that answer.

Read Deuteronomy 10:14-16.

The Lord's call on Israel. The Lord's call on us. He chose them and asked them to respond with hearts softened and responsive to Him.

In verse 16, He tells Israel to "circumcise your hearts." Circumcision was practiced by many nations in the ancient Near East (though it was not always done so as a sign of covenant with a God, as it was in Israel), so the concept would have been familiar to listeners even outside Israel.[167] Circumcision of the heart would call to mind a removal of the thickening/callousness around the heart, to render it more responsive.[168] Israel was being called to allow the Lord to remove their callous, stiff-necked ways, to be softened and more responsive to His leading and His love in and through them.

God had set His affection on Israel. He had loved them and chosen them, above all nations, to be His. The One who held the heavens and earth sought them as His own. He only longed that they would be softened to respond to His call on their hearts and their lives. And He considers and longs for the same for us as we are His, in Christ.

---

[167] Walton, John H., general editor. *Zondervan Illustrated Bible Backgrounds Commentary, Vol 1: Genesis, Exodus, Leviticus, Numbers, Deuteronomy*, 467.
[168] Berlin, Adele and Mark Zvi Brettler, *The Jewish Study Bible*, 369.

REFLECTION

We already considered how we, like Israel, may have been stiff-necked or stubborn toward the Lord. How might you allow the Lord to circumcise your heart? How might you allow Him to soften your heart toward Him and toward others? How do these concepts mutually work together?

"He set his affection on your ancestors and loved them, and he chose you." Have you struggled to accept this truth for yourself? The God of the universe—the One who owns heaven and earth and everything in it—has set His affection on your ancestors and loved them…and (my paraphrase) He has done the same for you. He has chosen you. Like Israel, He knows your failures. He knows your stubborn ways. He knows your wandering. But, like Israel, He also knows your great worth, and He knows your great witness and blessing to the nations of the world, that all may know the Lord. Respond to this truth below.

DAY FIVE

Justice for Fatherless, Widow, & Foreigner
(Deuteronomy 10:17-22)

*God's great love and call on Israel was not only for them,
but also for others less fortunate around them.
His love and justice were to flow to the fatherless,
the widow, and the foreigner.*

~•~•~

Read Deuteronomy 10:17-22.

The softening of Israel's heart would be foundational in helping them respond to God's call to extend love and grace to others in their midst. Moses took great care to remind Israel of the way God defends and cares for the less fortunate and often overlooked, and how He sees and cares for each of them.

Though Israel was set apart, she could not neglect the needs of those around her, particularly the needs of the foreigners who resided alongside them. (These would be different from the enemy nations that would have been driven out prior to their entering the land.) Israel had been rescued from the "house of slaves," and their own time in slavery should especially "enable them to act graciously toward the weak and vulnerable within their own society."[169]

In keeping with the heart of God and all of Scripture, and the very thesis of the book of Deuteronomy thus far, "complete love for God and for neighbor is the essence of what God requires of man."[170] And, similarly, in keeping with the heart of Deuteronomy, the sermons of Moses have revealed the "movement of being/becoming the family of Yahweh."[171] Love for God and love for their neighbor would mark this family as they reflected the character of their God in love and care for others.

Israel was called to fear the Lord and to serve Him. They were called to hold fast to Him and take their oaths in His name (revere Him alone). He was to be the one they praised, their

---
[169] Hess, Richard S. *The Old Testament: A Historical, Theological, and Critical Introduction*, 143.
[170] Schultz, Samuel J. *Deuteronomy: The Gospel of Love*, 47.
[171] Moberly, R.W.L. "Theological Interpretation of an OT book: A Response to Gordon McConville's Deuteronomy," 523.

God who had performed "great and awesome wonders" they had seen with their own eyes. The Lord had kept His promises. He had increased Israel and made them as numerous as the stars in the sky (Gen 22:17), and Israel would be walking in that truth. Their faithful God had loved and kept them, and now they had the opportunity to love Him and keep His commands, in love and faithfulness, in response.

REFLECTION

How can we reconcile this section and the concept of loving the foreigner with the call for destruction of other nations earlier in this book? How can the same God call for both?

In this section (v17), God is said to "show no partiality." We've seen this as a picture of His justice and goodness. How does this same God who shows no partiality (or favoritism) show His favor to Israel? How is that different from "favoritism?" How does the truth of God's lack of partiality or favoritism point to His justice for all? And how are we to reflect that character in our own lives (see James 2:1)?

How can you "hold fast" to God? What does this look like in one's daily practice? How is this (or is it) different from trusting or having faith in God and His promises?

WEEK NINE NOTES

WEEK TEN

Remember Today: Love the Lord & His Law

CHAPTER 11

We've come to the last week (and the last chapter) of our study. We've come to a crossroads for Israel, a place of recognizing the choice before them–the choice of blessing or curse–for their lifetime in the new land. We'll hear Moses' final words in this section of his sermons, as he prepares to share the core covenant laws with them (in chapters 12-26). He'll seek to best ensure they have been properly instructed and reminded of all the Lord would have him pass along before he dies in the wilderness and they take steps into their promise.

Let's join Moses in the call to choose!

DAY ONE

Love the Lord & Keep His Law
(Deuteronomy 11:1-7)

*As Moses prepares to introduce the law,
he repeats the cry to Israel to love the Lord
and remember all they had experienced.*

~•~•~

Read Deuteronomy 11:1-7.

Israel is called to remember all they had seen–the signs and wonders of deliverance and the signs and wonders of judgment–as motivation to keep the Lord's requirements, decrees, laws, and commands. It would be this "loyalty to the covenant that would provide the conditions for life in Canaan."[172]

Interestingly, within this chapter the pronoun "you" has become a plural "you," emphasizing the call to the community as a whole to keep all of these commands and to live this way.[173] (If you will remember, we learned together in week 4 that the "you" in the Ten Commandments was in the singular form, emphasizing the responsibility of each individual in keeping those commandments.) Israel was in a community-based culture at this time, so this isn't completely unexpected, but it may also ponit to the movement of the nation to more of a "family of Yahweh" as we considered last week.

In verse 2, Israel is called to remember the "mighty hand and outstretched arm" of their God with which He delivered them and disciplined them. We've seen this outstretched arm phrase throughout the book of Deuteronomy, but we haven't stopped to consider what it means. This expression would signify an "extension of power and authority" and was often used by Egyptian Pharaohs.[174] Isn't it interesting to consider an expression that had been used to describe the power and authority of their former oppressor was now used to describe their deliverer and trusted disciplinarian? Is this an additional picture of redemption?

---

[172] Berlin, Adele and Mark Zvi Brettler, *The Jewish Study Bible*, 370.
[173] Ibid.
[174] Walton, John H. *The IVP Bible Background Commentary: Genesis-Deuteronomy*, 232.

That same mighty hand and outstretched arm had been at work to overwhelm and bury the Egyptian army and ruin Pharaoh and his country, and to completely destroy them so Israel could make her escape and walk in the Lord's promises.

Interestingly, though, Moses reminds Israel that their children (current children) had not seen or experienced this for themselves. (Thus, they would need to be told, as we've previously considered.)

In verse 5, Moses reminds Israel that their children also did not see what the Lord had done when they arrived in the wilderness–revealing His presence in the cloud and the fire, providing manna and water, and also disciplining them. They specifically had not seen how the Lord had disciplined Dathan and Abiram.

Let's read this fascinating story.

Read Numbers 16:1-34.

Why had Moses brought up this particular discipline of the Lord? This was a picture of leaders within the tribes of Israel grumbling against Moses' leadership and against God Himself. This was a picture of the danger that comes with "groupthink" in general and with rebellion against the Lord and His leaders. Israel needed to remember this piece of their history and needed to be sure their children remembered as well. The Lord their God had done great things before them, in deliverance and discipline, and both warranted remembering as they entered the new land. "Memory serves as motivation" and these memories and motivations needed to be passed along to the new generation, so that they may love the Lord and keep His requirements as well.[175]

---

[175] Brueggeman, Walter. *Abingdon Old Testament Commentaries: Deuteronomy*, 135.

REFLECTION

This is our last time to consider this, but it bears repeating: how was Israel to love, remember, and obey their God? How are we to do the same?

Does anything in particular stand out to you in the story of Dathan and Abiram from Numbers 16:1-34? What might happen today if the land opened up and swallowed whole the people (and their families) that complained and grumbled about their leaders and about their God? (Would there be any of us left?!) How does this narrative serve as a warning against complaining or ridiculing those in authority over us?

How does the realization that all these verses utilize the plural "you" change the way you read them? (Or does it?) Try to keep your eyes open to this throughout this chapter and consider if it changes the way you read/hear the passages you are reading.

DAY TWO

Life in the New Land
(Deuteronomy 11:8-15)

Today's text seeks to strengthen the hearts and minds of Israel
before they go in and take over the land they've been given.
Moses gives Israel a greater picture of
the land and the care they will enjoy.

~ • ~ • ~

Read Deuteronomy 11:8-15.

In this section there is an oft-repeated word that demands Israel's attention. Do you see what it is?

What word is repeated throughout this section of chapter 11? _____

Israel had been hearing about the land their entire lives. It was a promise for which they had waited and hoped for across generations. And, as Moses continued to prepare them for what lie ahead, he offered them a view of the land for their hearts and minds to be encouraged and strengthened, and so be motivated to continue to obey the Lord and follow Him into this good land.

What did Moses say about the land they would enter?
- A land flowing with _____ and _____ (v9)
- A land… not like the land of _____ … where you _____ by foot (v10a)
- A land of _____ and _____ that drinks _____ from _____ (11b)
- A land the _____ _____ _____ cares for (v12a)

What is continually on it from the beginning of the year to the end? (v12b)

_____

How would these truths about the land encourage Israel's heart? _____
_____
_____

Moses proceeds in verses 13-15 to issue some "if-then" clause statements. Let's work through those statements below.

"If you _____—then I will

_____ so that

_____.

I will _____

and you will _____ and be _____.

There's that statement we've seen earlier—Israel would "eat and be satisfied." Had this been her experience in the wilderness wandering? Or had she been hungry and found herself wanting (whether in true hunger or simply craving)?

The Lord would provide all Israel would need in the new land. He would reveal Himself the sovereign God who controlled the rain and cared for Israel's every need. The nation that had spent 40 years wandering in the wilderness, hungry and thirsty, would settle into a land that would drink rain directly from heaven, and find themselves refreshed, full, and satisfied.

REFLECTION

We considered God's care and eye upon the good land. Does He still do this today? Have you considered God's care for you in these ways? How have you seen God's care and eye upon you lately?

WEEK TEN – DAY TWO

How would the mental picture of the good land, and its abundance and especially its irrigation and refreshing, be motivating to Israel as they prepared to go in and take possession of the land?

We have encountered many "repetitions" throughout the book of Deuteronomy, whether they be words, phrases, or concepts. Have you considered some of the reasons these repetitions would have been helpful to Israel? Beyond simply provoking an emotive response from the listeners, have you considered the importance they may have served to the remembrance of the texts in a culture still heavily reliant upon the oral tradition? How would the repetitions help these truths and promises be remembered and passed along to others (such as the next generation, as the charge is issued) more reliably?

DAY THREE

Be Careful Not to Forget
(Deuteronomy 11:16-21)

Whereas yesterday focused on the blessings for faithfully
obeying God's commands (with rain straight from God),
today will offer the curses for disobeying God and
outright turning away from Him to worship other gods.

Read Deuteronomy 11:16-21.

The refreshing and fruitful picture of the land we delighted in yesterday is not present in this passage. Instead, the heavens are shut up, so there is no rain, and the ground "will yield no produce." Israel "will soon perish." What has happened? What has changed?

Israel's obedience. In this passage, we are given the other side to yesterday's blessing passage. What a juxtaposition, to be sure! Israel's obedience (or considered here, disobedience) would have a bearing on how Israel would experience the land, and literally whether they would live or die.

As Moses closes this chapter, he will declare to Israel that he is setting before them a blessing and a curse, and he is prefacing that dynamic in the passages of yesterday and today. Israel has a role to play, and a choice to make, in how they will live.

In the second portion of this passage, did you see some familiar commands and encouragements?

What did Moses tell the Israelites to do in verses 18-20?

Where have you heard these before in our study?

Why would Moses repeat them here?

Moses did not want Israel to forget anything the Lord had taught them. Moses wanted the "days" of each Israelite and their children to "be many" in the new land.

REFLECTION

How can we help ourselves remember the commands and truths of God? Are there any spiritual disciplines we can practice to help with this?

Hardship and struggle are not always a sign of a curse or rebellious spirit. We have been reminded time and again in Scripture that we will endure suffering and we will face trouble, but that we can trust that God is at work and that He is producing in us a work that will lead to our good and His glory. How could we ever know if something in our lives is a curse or a trial ordained by God? (Hint: The book of Job holds a great example of a godly and righteous man who suffered many trials, of no cause or fault of his own, but who faithfully served God and refused to curse Him or stop following Him.)

Did you create a mezuzah in the extra exercise from Week Five? Have you found yourself remembering the Shema and the principles behind it when you see the mezuzah? Have you found yourself remembering God and your mission for Him as you leave your home to go out into the world? How has its presence affected you?

DAY FOUR

Walking in Grace & Victory
(Deuteronomy 11:22-25)

Moses continues to build his motivation and encouragement for Israel. This is a picture of blessing and victory that Israel surely could not ignore!

~•~•~

Read Deuteronomy 11:22-25.

Moses issued another "if-then" clause statement for Israel.

Let's consider what he offered them.

If you _____ — to _____ the Lord your God, to _____ _____ to him, and to _____ _____ to him–then the Lord will _____ and you will _____ _____. Every place you set your _____ will be _____, (22-24a)

No one will be able to _____ against _____. The Lord your God, as he promised you, will put the _____ _____ and _____ of you on the _____ land, wherever you go. (v25)

Wow. What more was there for the Lord to do to reveal His favor and blessing and might for Israel?!

REFLECTION

If Israel obeyed God, it is said that the Lord would put "terror and fear" of Israel on the whole land. Other nations, even those greater and stronger than Israel, would fear Israel, simply because of her God. How would this promise (and reality) stand in stark contrast to the terror and fear Israel felt regarding the stronger and greater nations they were supposed to drive out?

Israel's very feet would claim the land as theirs. Every place they set their foot would be theirs. How would this strengthen and quicken their steps? How would this help them to literally "walk in obedience" to the Lord?

God would bring terror and fear on the land around them, but Israel could have a confidence even without that promise. How could following God's commands give them a different confidence as they stepped forward to enter the new land? Have you experienced anything similar when you have been called to step out in faith? Have you been able to step out with greater confidence, knowing that you are seeking to follow God's command over your own desire?

DAY FIVE

Blessing or Curse: The Choice is Yours
(Deuteronomy 11:26-32)

We've arrived at the last day of the last week!
It's our final day together in study, and today we will hear
a charge of benediction from Moses to Israel, and so to us.

Let's begin.

Read Deuteronomy 11:26-32.

Moses set blessing and curse before Israel. He challenged them to recognize the choice they had, all related to their obedience to the Lord. Indeed, the covenant of God "is linked with the choice between obedience and disobedience and blessing and curse."[176] And, Moses is sure to remind Israel of that important truth.

Notably, Moses issued a command within these closing comments, to demand Israel remember these blessings and curses through ceremony once they had entered the new land. He prescribed the pronouncement of blessings and curses by calling for a ceremony in the valley between Mount Gerizim and Mount Ebal. These mountains were likely selected because they would represent the "center of the land" and a large portion of the land could be seen from these mountains.[177] They were to proclaim blessings while facing Mount Gerizim and curses while facing Mount Ebal. This physical exercise would serve to help them further remember the blessings and curses offered them by their God.

The closing verses of this chapter conclude the first large section of Moses' sermons, but also serve to provide an introduction of sorts for the next section of Deuteronomy, as Moses will begin to issue more specific commandments in chapters 12-26. (This is your invitation to join us for the second part of this study which will walk through those texts as well!)

---

[176] Ryken, Leland, James C. Wilhoit, and Tremper Longman, III. *Dictionary of Biblical Imagery*, 178.
[177] Walton, John H. *The IVP Bible Background Commentary: Genesis-Deuteronomy*, 233.

WEEK TEN – DAY FIVE

As we wrap up our time together, let's look at Moses' benediction to Israel and accept it as our own.

What is Moses setting before Israel? (v26)
a _____ and a _____

A blessing if you obey the commands of the Lord _____
A curse if you disobey the commands of the Lord _____

Which will Israel choose? Which will YOU choose? _____
_____

REFLECTION

Spoiler alert: Israel will respond with obedience (well, varied obedience over time, but early obedience to go into the land and take possession of it). How would the remembrance of Moses' sermons help them to keep "choosing" obedience and blessing over their lifetime?

In this text, Moses prescribed a ceremony to proclaim blessings and curses by physically turning toward one mountain or another with each proclamation, dependent upon whether it was a blessing or a curse. How would this help them to internalize and remember these blessings and curses? What type of visual reminder might those mountaintops offer the average Israelite on a daily basis in the future? Have you participated in an exercise or ceremony with the motivation of internalizing a concept or truth? How has that helped?

WEEK TEN NOTES

FINAL CONCLUSIONS

As we conclude this first leg of our study through Deuteronomy, take time to consider what you've learned and what you've enjoyed the most.

What are some things you've learned along the way?

What questions do you still have?

What do you hope to learn in the next section of Deuteronomy?

Has your time in Deuteronomy encouraged you to read other books or narratives within the Old Testament? Record what books or narratives you've visited as a result of this study. What have you learned in doing that?

How can you take the Deuteronomy story—the reminder to hear the Lord, to follow Him and to obey Him, as a work of heart in our lives—to others?

Author Brad Kelle says this about Deuteronomy: "Deuteronomy's final sermon has passed on the story of God's deliverance, covenant, and law to the new generation. We have a people who've been called, created, and formed to live as God's instrument of blessing, special possession, covenant people, priestly kingdom, glory-bearers, and holy nation for the sake of the world."[178]

That is what we've seen to be true in this study, and now it is my prayer that we will take this story with us as we live as a people who've been called to live the same.

Amen and Amen.

---

[178] Kelle, Brad E. *Telling the Old Testament Story: God's Mission and God's People.* (Nashville, TN: Abingdon Press, 2017), 109.

BIBLIOGRAPHY

Alexander, T. Desmond and David W. Baker, editors. *The Dictionary of the Old Testament: Pentateuch.* (Downers Grove, IL: InterVarsity Press, 2003).

Arnold, Bill T. and Bryan E. Beyer, editors. *Encountering the Old Testament: A Christian Survey.* (Grand Rapids, MI: Baker Books, 1999).

Arnold, Bill T. "The Love-Fear Antinomy in Deuteronomy 5-11." *Vestus Testamentum*, 61 no 4, 2011, 551-569.

Barker, Kenneth L. and John R. Kohlenberger, III, editors. *The Expositor's Bible Commentary, Abridged Edition: Old Testament.* (Grand Rapids, MI: Zondervan, 1994).

Ben-Gad HaCochen, Dr. David. "Where in the Transjordan Did Moses Deliver His Opening Address?" TheTorah.com. (2018). https://thetorah.com/article/where-in-the-transjordan-did-moses-deliver-his-opening-address

Berlin, Adele and Mark Zvi Brettler, editors. *The Jewish Study Bible, Second Edition.* (New York, NY: Oxford University Press USA, 2014).

Brueggeman, Walter. *Abingdon Old Testament Commentaries: Deuteronomy.* (Nashville, TN: Abingdon Press, 2001).

Connoway, Izaak J. and Johannes Malherbe. "The Proximity of Yahweh in Deuteronomy: A study of Key Phrases and Contexts" *Conspectus: The Journal of the South African Theological Seminary,* Oct 30 2020, 58-75.

Craigie, P.C. *The New International Commentary on the Old Testament: The Book of Deuteronomy.* (Grand Rapids, MI: William B. Eerdmans Publishing Company, 1976.)

Doty, Brant Lee. *Bible Study Textbook Series: Numbers.* (Joplin, MO: College Press, 1978).

Duguid, Iain M, general editor. *Numbers: God's Presence in the Wilderness.* (Wheaton, IL: Crossway Books, 2006).

Earl, Douglas S. "The Christian Significance of Deuteronomy 7." *Journal of Theological Interpretation*, 3 no 1, Spring 2009, 41-62.

Goldingay, John. *Do We Need the New Testament? Letting the Old Testament Speak for Itself.* (Downers Grove, IL: InterVarsity Press, 2015).

Hamilton, Victor P. *Handbook on the Pentateuch.* (Grand Rapids, MI: Baker Book House, 1982).

Hayes, Katherine M. "The Gift of Land: Instructions Included (Deuteronomy 7-8)." *The Bible Today*, 56 no 3, May-June 2018, 157-163.

Henry, Matthew. *A Commentary on the Whole Bible: Volume 1, Genesis to Deuteronomy.* (Old Tappan, NJ: Fleming H Revell Company,1883).

Hess, Richard S. *The Old Testament: A Historical, Theological, and Critical Introduction.* (Grand Rapids, MI: Baker Academic, 2016.

Hill, Andrew E. and John A. Walton, editors. *A Survey of the Old Testament, Third Edition.* (Grand Rapids, MI: Zondervan, 2009).

Holsteen, Nathan D. and Michael J. Svigel. *Exploring Christian Theology.* (Minneapolis, MN: Bethany House Publishers, 2014).

Kelle, Brad E. *Telling the Old Testament Story: God's Mission and God's People.* (Nashville, TN: Abingdon Press, 2017).

Kroeger, Catherine Clark and Mary J. Evans. *The IVP Women's Bible Commentary.* (Downers Grove, IL: InterVarsity Press, 2002).

Lange, John Peter, Phillip Schaff, and Wilhelm Julius Schroeder. *A Commentary on the Holy Scriptures: Deuteronomy.* (Bellingham, WA: Logos Bible Software, 2008).

Longman, Tremper III. *The Story of God Bible Commentary: Genesis.* (Grand Rapids, MI: Zondervan, 2016).

Martin, Oren R. *Bound for the Promised Land: The Land Promised in God's Redemptive Plan.* (Downers Grove, IL: InterVarsity Press, 2015).

Middlemas, Jill Anne. "Aniconism and Deuteronomy 4-5" *The Bible Today*, 56 no 3, May-June 2018, 151-156.

Millar, J. Gary. *Now Choose Life: Theology and Ethics in Deuteronomy.* (Downers Grove, IL: InterVarsity Press, 1998).

Moberly, R.W.L. "Theological Interpretation of an OT book: a Response to Gordon McConville's Deuteronomy." *Scottish Journal of Theology*, 56 no 4, 2003, 516-525.

Motyer, J.A. *The Message of Exodus: The Days of our Pilgrimage.* (Downers Grove, IL: InterVarsity Press, 2005).

NIV Cultural Study Backgrounds Bible. (Grand Rapids, MI: Zondervan, 2016).

Oberst, Bruce. *Bible Study Textbook Series: Deuteronomy.* (Joplin, MO: College Press, 1968).

Phetsanghane, Souksamay K. "What is the [hornet] of Exodus 23:28, Deuteronomy 7:20, and Joshua 24:12?" *Wisconsin Lutheran Quarterly,* 113 no 3, Summer 2016, 175-194.

Richter, Sandra L. *The Epic of Eden: A Christian Entry into the Old Testament.* (Downers Grove, IL: InterVarsity Press, 2008).

Ryken, Leland, James C. Wilhoit, and Tremper Longman, III. *Dictionary of Biblical Imagery.* (Downers Grove, IL: InterVarsity Press, 1998).

Scherman, Rabbi Nosson and Rabbi Meir Zlotovitz. *The Stone Edition: The Chumash.* (Brooklyn, NY: Mesorah Publications, Ltd, 2012).

Schultz, Samuel J. *Deuteronomy: The Gospel of Love.* (Chicago, IL: The Moody Bible Institute, 1971).

Smith, Richard L. "Such a Heart as This: The Intellectual Implications of Deuteronomy 5:29" *Evangelical Review of Theology*, vol 46, iss 1, Feb 2022, 24-37.

Tidball, Derek. *The Message of the Living God: His Glory, His People, His World.* (Downers Grove, IL: InterVarsity Press, 2000).

Walton, John H. *The IVP Bible Background Commentary: Genesis-Deuteronomy.* (Downers Grove, IL: InterVarsity Press, 1997).

Walton, John H. and D. Brent Sandy. *The Lost World of Scripture: Ancient Literary Culture and Biblical Authority*. (Downers Grove, IL: InterVarsity Press, 2013).

Walton, John H., general editor. *Zondervan Illustrated Bible Backgrounds Commentary, Vol 1: Genesis, Exodus, Leviticus, Numbers, Deuteronomy*. (Grand Rapids, MI: Zondervan, 2009).

Webb, William J. and Gordon K. Oeste. *Bloody, Brutal, and Barbaric? Wrestling with Troubling War Texts.* (Downers Grove, IL: InterVarsity Press, 2019).

Wiersbe, Warren W. *The Bible Exposition Commentary Old Testament: The Pentateuch, Genesis-Deuteronomy.* (Colorado Springs, CO: David C. Cook, 2001).

Wright, Christopher J.H. *Understanding the Bible Commentary Series: Deuteronomy.* (Grand Rapids, MI: Baker Books, 1996).

LEADER TIPS/HELPS

I'm excited you want to lead a women's Bible study and I'm honored that you've chosen this study of the book of Deuteronomy! Incredible things happen when women gather together with a shared desire to study God's Word and to grow in grace and truth together. It is my prayer that you and your group will experience this as well.

Here are a few "tips" to consider as you prepare to begin and lead your group.

1) Determine a day, time, and location that will work best for you and your group to meet regularly (ideally weekly), with the least disruptions to rhythm and transparent discussion.

2) Consider how you will share your group with others. How will you invite ladies to join you? Will you rely upon personal invites alone or will you promote the study through your local church? Allow plenty of time ahead of the study to get the word out to others.

3) Consider the necessary logistics and makeup of your group. Will you organize a bulk purchase of workbooks for participants or have ladies purchase their own workbooks? Will you offer childcare? Will you offer snacks? Will you need space to break into multiple smaller discussion groups? (See #4 below for more information about this) How will you handle individual prayer requests? (See #4 in Practical Tips/Suggestions for Small Group Discussion Leaders)

4) As you receive confirmations, recognize the potential need for co-leaders and additional discussion group leaders. It is preferable to keep the size of each discussion group at 10-12 ladies, if possible. This will help foster greater participation and opportunity for growth. Recruit additional ladies as appropriate.

5) Follow up with each participant to address any questions they may have. Help participants know what to expect for their schedules and help build excitement for the study. Encourage them to consider inviting a friend to join them for the study.

6) At the introductory session, offer administrative help (pass out workbooks if applicable, share weather/cancellation policies, confirm contact information, etc), facilitate introductions (consider having the ladies participate in this as a large group or within smaller circles as appropriate), share what a typical gathering will look like, and cover the introductory material/context information for the study. *If video teaching is available for this study, plan to watch the video together.

7) Over the course of the study weeks, be mindful to check in with ladies outside the formal gathering. Especially check in with those who have missed coming or who may have shared a heavier burden the previous week. Pray for each lady in your group by name often!

8) Be ready to see growth and change in hearts and minds. Be ready for ladies to grow closer to the Lord and closer to one another as they gather together to study. Delight in God's ways and God's care to knit hearts together in community and discipleship!

PRACTICAL TIPS/SUGGESTIONS FOR SMALL GROUP DISCUSSION LEADERS

1) Review the week's completed homework prior to meeting for discussion each week. Mark questions you want to be sure to ask the group to discuss. Always be ready to share your own answers to those questions (in case there is extended silence or reluctance to share), but know you may not need to share your own answer each time. Do allow yourself to become comfortable with silence and pause to allow ladies to follow a nudge to share; there is power in a silent pause.

2) Pray for your group. Ask the Holy Spirit to help you with question selections and with fostering an environment for sharing that is warm, hospitable, and safe. Ask the Lord to help you navigate and maintain gracious balance in groups that contain both eager and hesitant sharers. Have open eyes and an open heart to help encourage participation from each woman.

3) Take time to regularly remind the participants in your group of the commitment to create a safe place for sharing personal stories, personal struggles, and personal prayer requests. Knowing a space is safe goes a long way in fostering real heart and life change. A motto such as "What's shared [or prayed] in the group stays in the group" can help ladies remember the privilege and call to treat this group and this sharing of lives as sacred.

4) Prayer is an important piece of the discipleship process and our Christian lives. A Bible study group is an excellent space to practice and model prayer. That said, it can prove challenging to receive prayer requests verbally as part of the formal study.

One practical way to incorporate personal prayer for one another while still honoring the main focus of the Bible study group discussion may be the use of written prayer requests. An especially helpful approach I've personally adopted is to utilize index cards (or something similar). Encourage ladies to grab an index card each week upon arrival, write their name on it, and then write out their praises and prayer requests. Take a moment at the end of each discussion time to exchange these cards within the smaller discussion groups. This will allow each lady to be prayed for by name by another lady within the group. (I have suggested that, if ladies don't have something specific for which to ask for prayer, they can simply have their name on the card for another lady to pray for them more generally by name. This allows those less comfortable or familiar with prayer time to participate without feeling forced. Don't be surprised if you find ladies begin sharing requests over time as they experience the real benefit and blessing of prayer for one another!).

5) Create a roster for your small group. Share contact information (email/phone numbers) with one another so ladies can reach out to one another for encouragement and prayer between the weekly sessions. This is an incredible way to foster community and ministry to one another. (And it partners well with #4's focus on praying for one another. If the ladies know how to contact one another, they can feel more free to send a message to another lady for whom they're praying that week.)

6) Regarding incomplete or unfinished homework, determine how you want to address this. My personal suggestion is to encourage ladies to not allow a difficult week personally or in the homework to keep them from coming to gather with the ladies the following week. There is power in gathering together. There is an encouragement that is rich and timely that covers ground a strict focus on completed homework may not. There is growth and learning to be experienced in the listening to the discussion of others who worked through the questions (and there is an encouraging nudge to go back and finish the homework one missed!).

That said, I personally believe there is merit in adopting a policy that understands if a woman has any unanswered questions (due to not completing the homework for that date rather than simply because of confusion) she will refrain from sharing in the discussion for that question/those questions and instead simply listen. This can serve to protect the discussion time. This, of course, is a suggestion and personal approach, but I encourage you to consider how you want to handle this scenario within your group ahead of time. Discuss this with your lead facilitator to know their preferences for the group as well.

7) Have fun together! Consider offering snacks if practical (this is a great way to involve other ladies). Consider having a celebratory meal or outing to mark the study's completion. Be aware of opportunities to serve together in your churches and community. Take what you've learned beyond your gathering space and formal schedule.

SUGGESTED FLOW FOR WEEKLY GROUP STUDY MEETINGS

1) Welcome ladies each week!

2) Begin by gathering in small group discussion time. Facilitate sharing of answers in the discussion questions for each day (Note: consider prayerfully selecting one or two questions to highlight from each day to best foster discussion, connection, and growth).

3) Gather together in the larger group (if applicable with multiple discussion groups). Allow a few minutes (if able) to share any "aha!" moments revealed within the discussion time or consider any lingering questions.

4) *View supplemental video teaching assigned for that week. If time allows, consider followup closing comments and discussion before dismissal.

5) Pray over the large group before dismissal.

Repeat this pattern throughout the study. See the Lord move!

I'm praying for you as you step out in faith to lead and study with other ladies! I'll be asking the Lord to strengthen and direct you and to give you wisdom, love, and grace as you seek to serve Him and others in discipleship and love.

I'm eager to hear your stories of growth and transformation as you grow closer to God and to one another in this journey through God's Word!

I can't wait to see how the Lord helps you to remember His Word and His ways as He shapes and forms your heart to be more like His!

To God be all the glory and honor and praise! Amen!

APPENDIX/MAP[179]

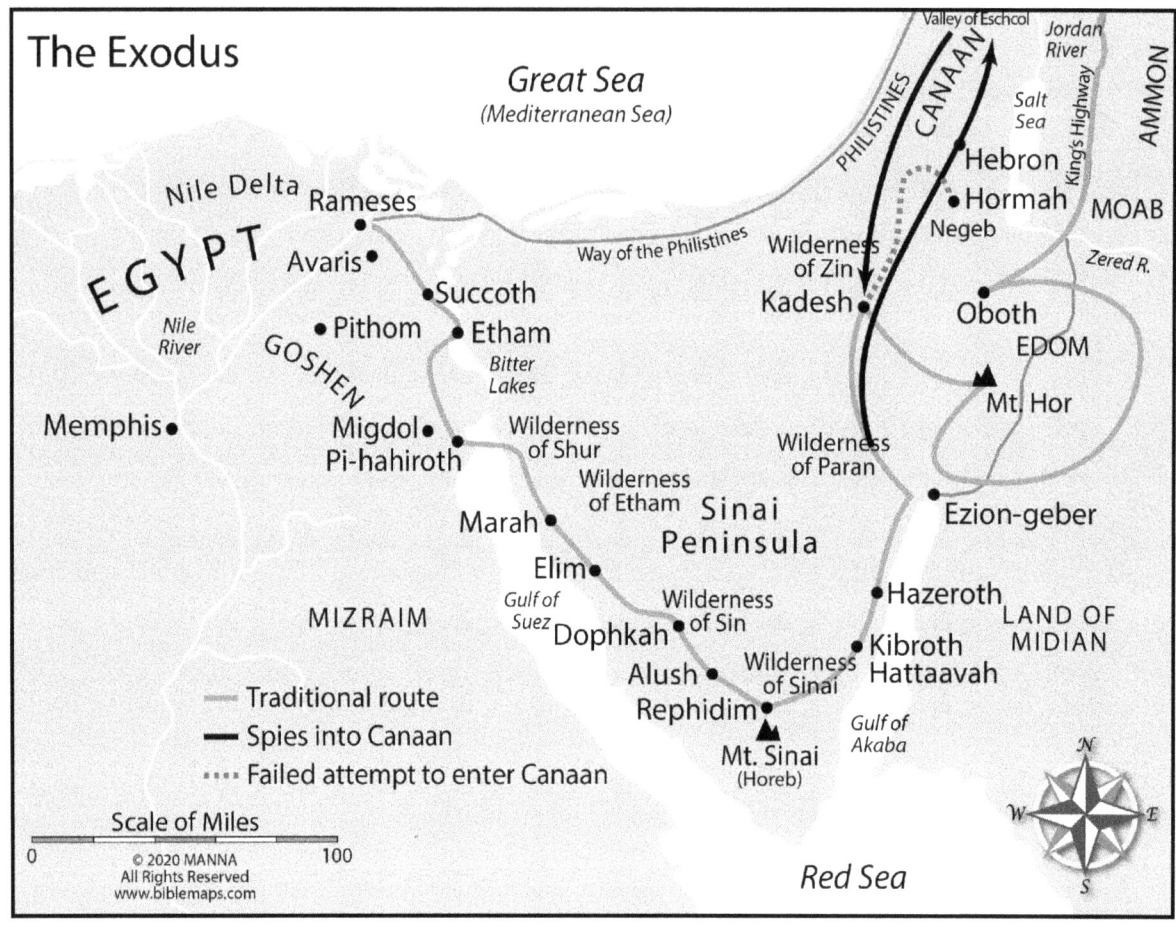

---

[179] The Exodus map used by permission from MANNA Bible Maps 18410 Standwick Drive, Louisville, KY 40245, Phone: 630-728-8828, Web: www.biblemaps.com.

www.ingramcontent.com/pod-product-compliance
Lightning Source LLC
Chambersburg PA
CBHW060922170426

43191CB00025B/2453